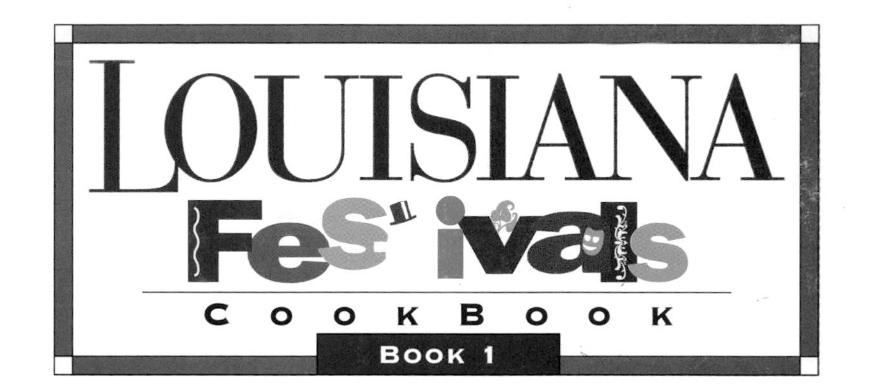

Distributed by
GULF PUBLISHING COMPANY
P.O. Box 2608
Houston, TX 77252-2608 USA

Acadian House
PUBLISHING
LAFAYETTE, LOUISIANA

ABOUT THE COVER: Louisiana is a land of cultural richness and diversity, and nowhere is this reflected better than in her food and festivals. Included in this cultural gumbo are more than 300 festivals of all sizes and styles, including those depicted here, namely the Alligator Festival of Franklin, the Blueberry Festival of Mansfield, the Corn Festival of Bunkie and the Frog Festival of Rayne.

--Illustration by Tony O. Champagne,
New Orleans, Louisiana

ABOUT THIS BOOK...
"Louisiana Festivals Cookbook (Book 1)" is the first in a continuing series of cookbooks featuring prize-winning recipes from the cooking contests sponsored by various festivals throughout the state. In addition to having recipes from 25 festivals, the book includes stories about each of these festivals, paintings reflecting each festival's theme, and specific information on the nutrients contained in each recipe, such as calorie count, carbohydrates, fat content, and the like.

Library of Congress Catalogue Card Number: 92-71567

ISBN: 0-925417-10-6

♦ Published by Acadian House Publishing, Lafayette, Louisiana
♦ Graphic design by Tom Sommers, Crowley, Louisiana
♦ Color illustrations by Tony O. Champagne, New Orleans, Louisiana
♦ Black-and-white illustrations by Sheila Macdonald, Houston, Texas
♦ Color separations by Toucan Scan, Portland, Oregon
♦ Printed by Arcata Graphics, New Canton, Tennessee

Introduction

The magic of the festivals, the excellence of the food

Louisiana's unique culture has been the subject of thousands of newspaper and magazine articles since the early 1970s, and no two aspects of this culture have drawn the attention of reporters more than the food and festivals.

Feature story writers from every corner of the modern world have visited the state to cover the festivals (and have fun doing it) and to write about the food (and enjoy eating it). Whether they came primarily to do their jobs or to personally experience the magic of the festivals and the excellence of the cuisine is altogether debatable!

Even if they came mostly to enjoy themselves, who could blame them?

After all, there's no place on earth quite like Louisiana when it comes to food and festivals! Why, there are more than 300 festivals in this state, ranging from the International Rice Festival in Crowley to the Blueberry Festival in Mansfield, from the Soybean Festival in Jonesville to the Great French Market Tomato Festival in New Orleans, from the Yambilee in Opelousas to Contraband Days in Lake Charles.

What goes on at these festivals is enough to keep anyone's attention for indefinite periods of time. There are common events like parades, carnivals, cooking contests, beauty pageants, sack races, face-painting and pie-eating. There are also more exotic events like crawfish, crab, frog and lizard races; catfish-skinning, shrimp-peeling and oyster-shucking competitions; duck-calling, calf-calling and hog-calling contests; not to mention cracklin-cooking contests and old-fashioned hog-butcherings, known in these parts as *boucheries*.

The Louisiana festival has proven to be fertile ground for the imagination of people with a penchant for humor and whimsey. Some of those in charge of creating special events for the festivals have come up with the idea of dressing the animals in human clothing or making little animated characters out of vegetables. As a result, you'll find frogs dressed up like people for the Frog Festival in Rayne and little pigs dressed like school children for the Swine Festival in Basile. In Opelousas at the Yambilee one can find a line up of little characters

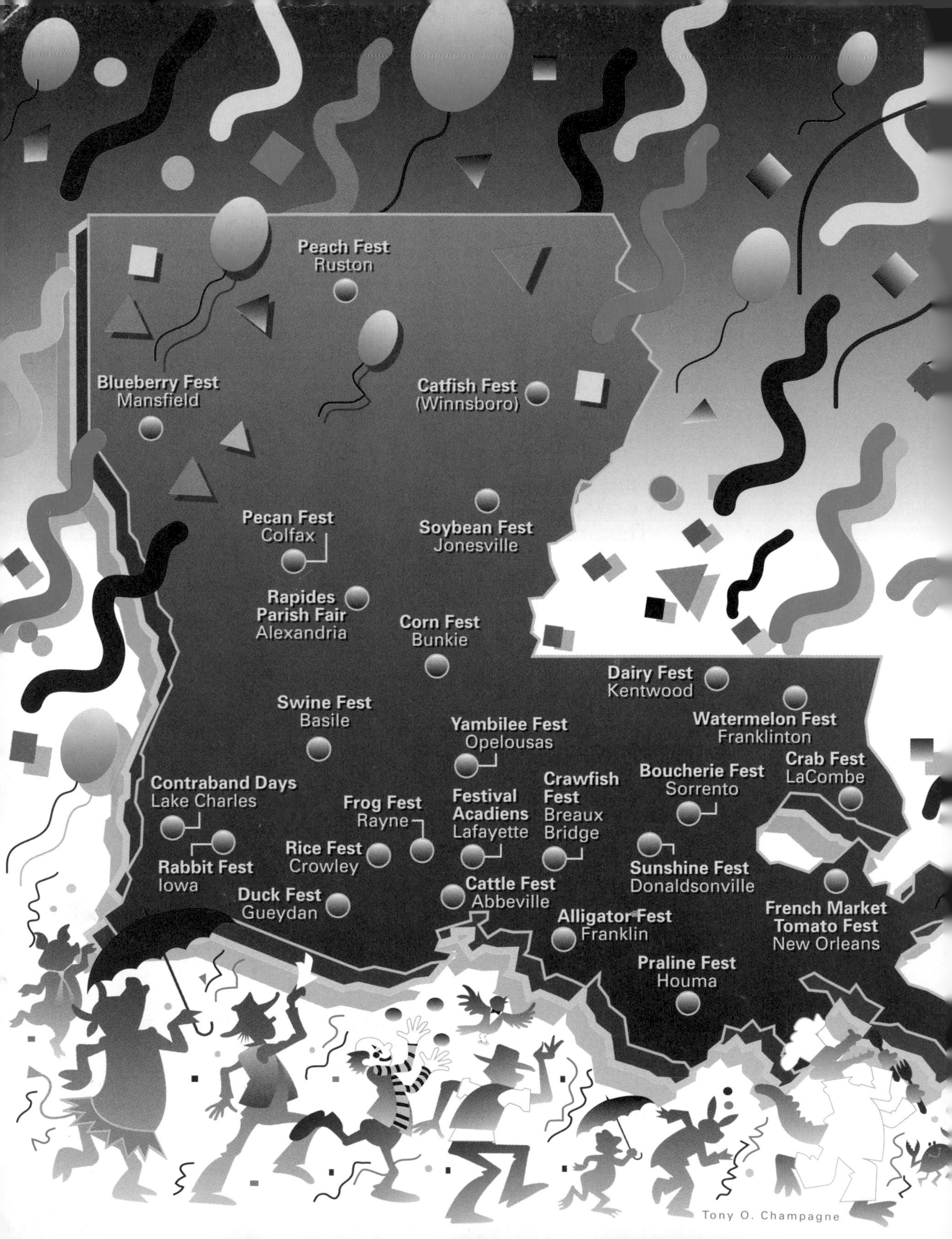

Peach Fest
Ruston
Blueberry Fest
Mansfield
Catfish Fest
(Winnsboro)
Pecan Fest
Colfax
Soybean Fest
Jonesville
Rapides
Parish Fair
Alexandria
Corn Fest
Bunkie
Dairy Fest
Kentwood
Swine Fest
Basile
Yambilee Fest
Opelousas
Watermelon Fest
Franklinton
Crab Fest
LaCombe
Contraband Days
Lake Charles
Boucherie Fest
Sorrento
Crawfish
Fest
Breaux
Bridge
Frog Fest
Rayne
Festival
Acadiens
Lafayette
Rice Fest
Crowley
Rabbit Fest
Iowa
Sunshine Fest
Donaldsonville
Cattle Fest
Abbeville
Duck Fest
Gueydan
Alligator Fest
Franklin
French Market
Tomato Fest
New Orleans
Praline Fest
Houma
Tony O. Champagne

known as "Yamimals," which are yams made to look like animals with the help of pipe cleaners, tooth picks, feathers and construction paper.

Most festivals in Louisiana were invented to call attention to and promote a crop or animal important to the local economy. Others were conceived as a way to raise funds for good causes, such as building a church hall or sending economically disadvantaged children to summer camp. Still others were created just for the fun of it.

The various reasons for which some of these festivals came into being, and the manner in which they were initiated, make up a colorful bit of Louisiana lore. Take the Blueberry Festival in Mansfield, for example. A two-acre patch of blueberries planted by an elderly couple is what launched the Blueberry Festival and the DeSoto Parish blueberry industry, which is now producing a million pounds of blueberries a year. The Sunshine Festival in Donaldsonville was started to bring some sunshine back into the community after the state's oil industry went into a deep and prolonged slump, starting in the early 1980s. (The City of Donaldsonville, incidentally, sits at the foot of the Sunshine Bridge over the Mississippi River. The bridge was named for the song "You Are My Sunshine," written by country singer and former Louisiana Governor Jimmie Davis.) The Great New Orleans French Market Tomato Festival was created as a means of reminding local folks that the historic French Market, situated at the edge of the French Quarter, is not only a tourist attraction but also a great place to shop for fresh fruits and vegetables, jewelry, clothing, etc.--and has been for more than 200 years.

Speaking of fresh foods, it is common knowledge that Southerners have the well-deserved reputation for knowing how to cook. And no one does it better than the women (and some men) who run the kitchens in Louisiana homes.

Jambalaya, crawfish pie and filé gumbo are among the specialties in the Cajun country, while shrimp Creole, red beans and rice, and okra and tomatoes are often associated with New Orleans. Many of the classic Southern dishes, such as fried chicken, corn bread and peach pie, are often prepared in north and central Louisiana.

While it is true that different cooking traditions were developed in different parts of the state, it is also true that the people of each of these areas have incorporated the specialties of other areas into their own cooking repertoire. What's good in one part of the state has been "borrowed" by people in other parts. So, much of what is considered

Louisiana cooking is, in reality, a blending of the best elements of several culinary styles.

This cookbook reflects this fact, as it features recipes from north and central Louisiana, from the Cajun country of south Louisiana, and from New Orleans. In it, you will find a cornucopia of good things to eat, including pork roast, veal supreme, stuffed peppers, baked duck, rabbit smothered in onion gravy, boudin sausage, cabbage rolls, Creole steak and chili. Some of the seafood dishes in the book are crawfish etouffee, grilled shrimp, stuffed flounder, catfish gumbo, crawfish fettuccine, and Louisiana seafood sauce piquante. There is a variety of baked vegetables plus fried green tomatoes, fried eggplant, sweet potato pie and a number of casseroles made with vegetables and meats. The book will also inform the reader on how to make blueberry cobbler, creamy pralines with pecans, homemade strawberry ice cream, pecan pie, watermelon punch, chocolate fudge, divinity, coconut pound cake, German chocolate cake, and other dishes that will make the mouth water.

Louisiana is, indeed, one of the most unique and culturally diverse states in the union. Nowhere is this more evident than in her food and festivals.

The excellence of the food and the mirth and magic of the festivals are the drawing cards for hundreds of reporters every year and hundreds of thousands of other visitors in search of the finer things of life.

--TRENT ANGERS
Editor & Publisher

Preface

A cookbook from Lou Ana Gardens and the kitchens of Louisiana

Each of the recipes in this book was prepared with tender loving care in someone's kitchen in Louisiana. Many were prize-winners in cooking contests held in conjunction with festivals in various parts of the state. Others can best be described simply as excellent recipes submitted by some of Louisiana's best cooks and chefs.

We at Lou Ana Gardens and Lou Ana Foods, Inc. are pleased to bring you this unique collection of recipes that has never been available to a wide number of cooks and food-lovers until now.

This is the first in a series of cookbooks featuring prize-winning or otherwise outstanding Louisiana recipes that will be presented by Lou Ana Gardens, a sister company to Lou Ana Foods, Inc., of Opelousas, La. Other cookbooks on a wide range of subjects are on the drawing board. We intend to provide the consumer with a good variety of tasty, well-tested recipes for quite some time to come.

In addition to sharing recipes, this cookbook has a number of other purposes.

First and foremost, we want to give the rest of the nation and the world a glimpse into Louisiana's rich and varied culture. From the swamps of the south to the peach orchards of the north, Louisiana is a veritable cultural gumbo flavored with ethnic ingredients from a wide variety of countries. Quite candidly and unabashedly, we want to promote the virtues of this state, which has been Lou Ana's home since 1894.

Secondly, we believe a cookbook should provide more than recipes. This book has been designed with eye-catching art work, narratives on each festival and a format that makes it at home on the coffee table as well as in the kitchen. It may even serve as a travel guide. It is our feeling that cooking should be fun, and we hope this book makes time spent in the kitchen more enjoyable.

Finally, we at Lou Ana Foods, Inc. want to be recognized by the public as a manufacturer and purveyor of splendid culinary ingredients that will enhance any cooking endeavor.

Our goal at Lou Ana Gardens and Lou Ana Foods is to continue to provide the home cook as well as the professional chef with high-quality food ingredients that will enhance any culinary effort. We aim at excellence.

Theodore G. Schad, Jr.

Theodore G. Schad, Jr.

Chairman of the Board & Chief Executive Officer
Schad Industries, Inc.
Lou Ana Foods, Inc.
Lou Ana Gardens, Inc.

A WORD ABOUT LOU ANA GARDENS

Lou Ana Gardens, Inc. is a sister company to Lou Ana Foods, Inc. of Opelousas, La., founded in 1989 by the parent company, Schad Industries, Inc. In addition to publishing cookbooks, Lou Ana Gardens is engaged in horticultural pursuits. The company's first venture was the growing of flowers for the cut flower market, a project that continues to meet with success.

In the future, Lou Ana Gardens will also produce exotic vegetables, herbs and spices. The consumer will benefit from the company's research and production as new and exciting food products, from seasonings to sauces, become available.

Foreword

Selecting, testing and analyzing the recipes for this cookbook

The effort to produce this cookbook began in 1987 when festival coordinators throughout Louisiana were asked to submit top-flight recipes for use in the book. They responded with enthusiasm, sending in recipes for a wide array of excellent-tasting foods. Many of these were prize-winning recipes from cooking contests held in conjunction with their respective festivals.

The recipes were then sent to Louisiana Tech University in Ruston for testing and for adjustments, where needed. The work was done in the Food Science Laboratory in the College of Human Ecology at the university. Numerous student laboratory employees worked on the project under the direction of Dr. Shirley Reagan, Professor of Food and Nutrition.

The recipe-evaluation process was as follows:

--Each recipe was prepared twice as submitted.

--If there were any quality problems (flavor, texture, color, etc.) adjustments in ingredients and/or procedures were made to correct the problems.

--The recipe was again prepared twice using conventional volume measurements.

--These measurements were then converted to grams to ensure exactness in the final testing and evaluation stage.

--Each recipe was again produced four times using gram measurements. Masses of ingredient combinations and the final product were determined for use in nutrient calculations. Volume measurements of final products were made for use in determining number of servings.

--Ten sensory panel members tasted the dish and completed an evaluation form each of the four times the product was prepared for the final evaluation.

At this point, and at various other points during the process, some recipes were eliminated from consideration for use in the cookbook.

Once the testing and final writing of the recipes was completed, the recipes were sent to Pennington Biomedical Research Center at LSU in Baton Rouge for nutrient analysis. This was done by Dr. Catherine Champagne, PhD, LDN, RD and Nutrient Data Systems Scientist, using the Extended Table of Nutrient Values. (This nutrient data base was developed by Dr. Margaret Moore of New Orleans; it is the data base that has been used for the well-known Bogalusa Heart Study.)

Dr. Champagne produced an analysis on 105 nutrient-related variables, seven of the most important of which are presented in this cookbook, along with the recipes, as a service to today's health-conscious consumer. The balance of the information derived from the nutrient analysis is on file at Lou Ana Foods in Opelousas and is available to health professionals upon request.

Acknowledgements

The publisher acknowledges with gratitude the following people for their work on this project:

The festival organizers throughout Louisiana who provided excellent recipes, as well as cooperation with the reporters gathering information for stories about the various festivals.

The faculty and staff at Louisiana Tech University who patiently tested and standardized the recipes under the direction of Dr. Shirley Reagan.

Dr. Catherine Champagne at Pennington Biomedical Research Center at LSU in Baton Rouge, who did the nutrient analysis of the recipes and provided the nutrient data which appears below the recipes in the following pages.

Judith Sylvester, corporate nutritionist at Lou Ana Foods from 1985 to 1990, who procured the recipes, coordinated the project between Lou Ana Foods, Louisiana Tech and LSU, and performed countless professional and administrative tasks necessary to get an abundance of well-written, well-tested recipes into the hands of the publisher.

Buz Carter, Manager, Retail Marketing, Lou Ana Foods, who helped steer the book through the maze of options and the network of deadlines which are involved in a project of this nature.

Tony O. Champagne, the artist who painted the cover and all of the color illustrations appearing inside the book, for his patience and the painstaking efforts he made in producing these works of art.

Amanda Griffin, for her able assistance in rendering the final version of the festival stories.

The staff of Acadian House Publishing, including Tom Sommers, who designed and produced the book; Doug Nix, who did the typesetting; Blake Devillier and Lisa Topham, the proofreaders; and Christine Trumps, who patiently assisted the publisher in dozens of ways from the start of the project to the finish.

Table of Contents

About the Artist...

TONY O. CHAMPAGNE of New Orleans, one of Louisiana's most prolific and extensively published artists, designed and illustrated the cover of this book as well as all of the color paintings inside the book.

A master of the airbrush medium, which he used in illustrating this book, he also uses pencil, pen & ink, wash, watercolor, acrylics, flurographics and computer graphics, depending on the work at hand.

Since 1974, when he graduated from Tulane University with a Bachelor of Fine Arts Degree, he has been a designer and illustrator for the New Orleans *Times-Picayune.* His works have been used to illustrate articles in the sports, travel, living and food sections, as well as for numerous covers of *TV Focus* magazine, which appears weekly in the newspaper.

Champagne is the official illustrator for the New Orleans Saints Hall of Fame in Kenner, La. One of the paintings he did for the Hall of Fame, featuring place-kicker Tom Dempsey, was used on the cover of a book commemorating the team's 25th anniversary in 1991. He also painted the 1990 Crescent City Classic poster, as well as the 1990 Mardi Gras poster, commissioned by Accent Annex of New Orleans.

A two-time Addy Award-winner for excellence in advertising design and illustration, his graphics has appeared in ads for McDonald's, Popeye's, LSU, the University of New Orleans, Louisiana Power & Light and the New Orleans Tourist Commission.

Champagne's work has appeared in nationally circulated publications such as the *Los Angeles Times*; *The Quill*, a journalism trade journal; and *The Black Collegian*, a magazine about Black colleges and students.

The artist is currently an annual staff member of the internationally acclaimed Poynter Institute for Media Studies in St. Petersburg, Florida. He has lectured extensively in the New Orleans school system, in art groups and on college campuses.

The Reporters...

The information used in preparing the festival stories contained in this book was gathered by 17 reporters, all of them Louisiana residents. They are: **Trent Angers** of Lafayette (Yambilee); **Patricia Chambers** of New Iberia (Cattle Festival); **C. Richard Cotton** of Brittany (Sorrento Boucherie and Sunshine Festival); **Bob Dailey** of Lafayette (Breaux Bridge Crawfish Festival); **Verdis Dowdy** of Alexandria (Rapides Parish Fair and Soybean Fest); **Mary Alice Fontenot** of Lafayette (International Rice Festival); **Billy Gunn** of Lafayette (Pecan Festival); **Angelique Lastrapes** of New Orleans (Bayou Lacombe Crab Fest and Greater New Orleans French Market Tomato Festival); **Rosemary Ludeau** of Ville Platte (Swine Fest and Kentwood Dairy Fest); **Jane Menard** of Church Point (Watermelon Fest and Blueberry Fest); **Jacquie Niebert** of Bunkie (Corn Festival); **Lois Petitjean** of Rayne (Frog Festival); **Don Shoopman** of New Iberia (Alligator Festival); **Christine Smith** of DeRidder (Rabbit Festival and Contraband Days); **Suzanne S. Smith** of Lafayette (Duck Festival); **Carol Stubbs** of Lafayette (Peach and Catfish Festivals and *Festivals Acadiens*); and **Evelyn Truxillo** of Gray (Praline Festival).

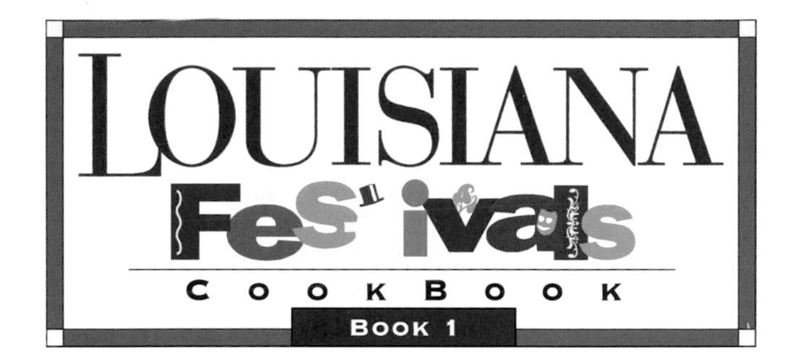
LOUISIANA
Festivals
CookBook
Book 1

tony Q. CHAMPAGNE

Mansfield

Blueberries Put Mansfield on Festival Map

A two-acre patch of blueberries planted by an 80-year-old couple started DeSoto Parish's blueberry industry and the Louisiana Blueberry Festival.

Jay and Kay Jones, an elderly couple who lived in DeSoto Parish for a few years, were the first to plant blueberries there. Although the couple later moved to Colorado for health reasons, their blueberries, planted in 1980, remained.

Today the parish is producing a million pounds of blueberries a year and hosting a three-day Blueberry Festival on the third weekend in June. The festival, which has attracted as many as 30,000 visitors in a single year, was started in 1987.

Blueberries have only recently been introduced as a crop in the South. They contain fiber, few calories and are easy to propagate. The plants themselves prefer acid soil and plenty of moisture. Many acres considered worthless for agriculture can yield profitable crops of blueberries.

Local farmers and cooks have created a variety of ways to use the versatile berries. Blueberry drinks, syrups, lemonade, daiquiris, eggnog, butter, breads, pies and even pizza are just a few of their recipes, many of which can be sampled during the festival weekend.

Fried blueberry pie is one of the festival's most popular offerings.

In addition to baking contests, the festival features volleyball tournaments, games and crafts, all on the courthouse square in Mansfield.

The festival is sponsored by International Paper and local banks and businesses. Jay and Kay Jones, who unknowingly helped create the festival, returned for the first one and were crowned King and Queen Blu-Dah in honor of their contribution.

Blueberry-Oatmeal Cookies

- 1 cup butter
- 3/4 cup sugar
- 3/4 cup dark brown sugar, packed
- 2 eggs, beaten-well
- 2 1/4 cups all-purpose flour
- 2 cups regular oats
- 1/4 teaspoon salt
- 1 teaspoon baking powder
- 1/2 teaspoon baking soda
- 2 teaspoons cinnamon
- 1/2 teaspoon nutmeg
- 1 cup blueberries, fresh
- 1 cup chopped pecans

1. Preheat oven to 350 degrees F. Grease cookie sheets.
2. Cream together butter and sugars.
3. Add eggs. Beat well.
4. Mix flour, oats, salt, baking powder, baking soda, cinnamon and nutmeg.
5. Add dry ingredients to creamed mixture.
6. Fold in blueberries and chopped pecans.
7. Drop batter by the teaspoonful onto greased baking sheets.
8. Bake 12 to 14 minutes.

Yield: 4 dozen cookies (each about 4 inches in diameter)

Each cookie contains:

Calories	111	Protein	1.6 g
Carbohydrate	13.6 g	Sodium	70 mg
Total Fat	5.9 g	Cholesterol	22 mg
		Saturated Fat	2.6 g

Jill Frazier

Easy Blueberry Cobbler

6 tablespoons butter

4 cups blueberries, fresh or frozen

1 1/2 cups sugar, divided

1 cup all-purpose flour

1 tablespoon baking powder

2/3 cup milk

1. Preheat oven to 350 degrees F.
2. Melt butter in a 9" x 13" baking dish.
3. Heat blueberries with 1/2 cup of sugar in a 2-quart saucepan until boiling.
4. Mix flour, remaining 1 cup of sugar, and baking powder. Add milk and mix well.
5. Pour batter over melted butter.
6. Pour blueberries over batter.
7. Bake for 30 to 35 minutes.

Makes 12 servings

Each serving contains:

Calories	221	Protein	1.9 g
Carbohydrate	40.3 g	Sodium	110 mg
Total Fat	6.5 g	Cholesterol	18 mg
		Saturated Fat	3.9 g

Francis Brasher

Tony O. CHAMPAGNE

Bringing Sunshine to Donaldsonville

Donaldsonville

Back in the 1980s when Louisiana's oil industry bottomed out, civic leaders in Donaldsonville decided something was needed to bring a little sunshine back into the community.

As one resident pointed out, not much of note had taken place in Donaldsonville since the building of the famous Sunshine Bridge. Despite being the State Capital for a brief period in the 1800s, Donaldsonville remained a quiet community on the Mississippi River between New Orleans and Baton Rouge.

So, it was in 1984 that the local Chamber of Commerce started the annual Sunshine Festival, which has grown into a delightful down home celebration that attracts 5,000 to 10,000 visitors every October.

Celebrants dance to rock, blues, country and Cajun tunes at the festival site on Railroad Avenue. A big draw is the Gospel Tent, where audience and preacher participate with great fervor.

If LSU is playing football on the Saturday of the festival, many festival-goers are content to while away the afternoon around a large-screen television watching the Tigers. Children can line up for the midway rides or watch a dog show, clown or magic act on the entertainment stage.

The festival's main event takes place on Sunday when local cooks compete in the Wild Game and Seafood Cookoff. This is not "camp food" (something you might find on the stove at a hunting camp), organizers point out, but gourmet fare that earns the champion a year's worth of bragging rights.

Festival proceeds go to such community organizations as the volunteer fire department, the schools and the handicapped citizens group.

Louisiana Seafood Sauce Piquante

1 1/2 cups Lou Ana Vegetable Oil

2 cups all-purpose flour

2 cups chopped onion

2 garlic cloves, minced

1/2 cup chopped green bell pepper

1/4 cup chopped celery

2 pounds catfish fillets

1 can (8 ounces) Rotel tomatoes with chilies, diced

1 can (4 ounces) tomato sauce

1 can (10 3/4 ounces) cream of mushroom soup

2 quarts water

1 pound peeled raw shrimp

1 pound lump crabmeat

1. In heavy sauce pot (10 quarts) make a roux by combining oil and flour over medium heat, stirring constantly until golden brown.
2. Add onion, garlic, green bell pepper, and celery to roux and continue cooking for about 15 minutes.
3. Cut 1 pound of catfish into small pieces and add to roux.
4. After about 5 minutes, add Rotel tomatoes, tomato sauce, cream of mushroom soup, and water.
5. Allow to simmer for about 1 hour, stirring often to avoid sticking.
6. While sauce is simmering, bake remaining 1 pound of catfish on sheet pan for 20 minutes at 400 degrees F. (This will firm up the catfish.)
7. At the end of the 1 hour of simmering, add shrimp, catfish (baked) and lump crabmeat.
8. Continue cooking for approximately 20 minutes or until catfish, shrimp, and crab are done.

9. Add seasoned salt, salt and pepper.
10. Green onion and parsley should be added about 15 minutes before sauce piquante is done.
11. Serve over rice.

Yield: 18 cups
Makes 18 servings

Each serving contains:

Calories	370	Protein	19.6 g
Carbohydrate	17.9 g	Sodium	409 mg
Total Fat	25.2 g	Cholesterol	78 mg
		Saturated Fat	4.9 g

Jerry Folse

1 tablespoon seasoned salt

1/2 teaspoon salt

1/2 teaspoon black pepper

1 cup chopped green onion

1/3 cup parsley

TONY O. CHAMPAGNE

Think of the New Orleans French Market as a Place to Shop

Stalls filled with fresh fruits and vegetables, art items and a lot of things in between can be found at the French Market, located on the edge of New Orleans' famous French Quarter.

On the first weekend in June, visitors to "the city that care forgot" will also find a robust festival in progress at the French Market. The festival celebrates not only the wonderful food and music found in the French Quarter, but also the Creole vegetable season.

The star of the early summer growing season is the Creole tomato, which is valued by area chefs for its distinctive flavor, and grown along the reclaimed Mississippi Delta.

Lou Costa, director of the French Market Company, dreamed up the festival in 1987 as a way to remind New Orleanians that the French Market is a good place to shop for food, not just a tourist stop.

The most popular attraction of the festival is the cooking demonstrations put on by area chefs and cookbook authors.

But, the soft, sultry strains of New Orleans' jazz can also be heard at the festival via a schedule of live concerts throughout the weekend.

Each year something new is added to the festival. One year, to the delight of the children present, "Little Red Riding Hood" was performed, and the heroine carried tomatoes in her basket instead of goodies.

The festival site includes the entire French Market, starting at Jackson Square and ending at Esplanade Avenue. Organizers estimate that 50,000 visitors attend the festival.

Creole Tomato Chelsea

6 slices fresh regular tomatoes, cut 3/4 to 1 inch thick

3 tablespoons balsamic or good red wine vinegar

1/4 cup butter, softened

1/2 tablespoon dried or 3 tablespoons fresh basil

1 1/2 teaspoons finely chopped garlic

1/2 teaspoon salt

1/4 teaspoon black pepper

1 tablespoon chopped parsley

1 1/2 tablespoons Parmesan cheese

1. Place slices of tomatoes on a plate and pour vinegar on top.
2. Allow the vinegar to soak into the slices approximately 10 minutes.
3. Meanwhile, combine the softened butter with fresh basil, garlic, salt, pepper, and parsley.
4. Spread an equal amount of the butter mixture on each tomato slice. (This may be done in advance.)
5. To pan fry, place tomatoes with butter side down in a preheated pan.
6. Cook for 2 1/4 minutes.
7. Flip over and cook an additional two minutes.
8. Sprinkle with Parmesan cheese and serve immediately.
9. To cook in the oven, bake at 375 degrees with butter side up for 7 to 9 minutes.
10. Sprinkle with Parmesan cheese and serve immediately.

Yield: Six slices
Makes 3 servings (2 slices per serving)

Each serving contains:

Calories	181	Protein	2.7 g
Carbohydrate	8.1 g	Sodium	604 mg
Total Fat	16.6 g	Cholesterol	44 mg
		Saturated Fat	10.1 g

Chef Tom Gerlak
Doubletree Hotel, New Orleans

Chicken Costa

2 pounds raw shrimp, in shells

3 tablespoons Lou Ana Vegetable Oil

1 1/2 cups chopped onion

1 cup Creole tomatoes, peeled and seeds removed

1 pound chicken bones

1 cup white wine

4 cups water

2 deboned chicken breast halves

3 egg whites

1 cup heavy cream

1 teaspoon salt

1/2 teaspoon black pepper

6 deboned chicken breast halves

1. Preheat oven to 375 degrees F.
2. Peel shrimp and reserve peels.
3. Sauté shrimp peelings in saucepan with oil and chopped onion until the onion is caramelized.
4. Add tomatoes, chicken bones, white wine, and cover with water.
5. Simmer 30 minutes and then strain. Cook until slightly thickened for sauce.
6. In food processor, make mousse with two breast-halves of chicken, egg whites, and cream.
7. Stir in shrimp, salt and pepper, mixing well.
8. Flatten remaining six chicken breast-halves by pounding. To the center of the chicken breast, add mousse with shrimp tails. Roll jellyroll-style and wrap in aluminum foil.
9. Bake 20 minutes in oven. Slice each roll into medallions. Cover serving plate with sauce. Place medallions on top of the sauce.

Note: Crawfish may be used in the place of shrimp.

Makes 6 servings (1 roll with 2 1/2 tablespoons of sauce per serving)
Left over: 2 1/2 to 3 cups of sauce; 2 1/4 cups of mousse

Each serving contains:

Calories	399	Protein	60.8 g
Carbohydrate	2.7 g	Sodium	633 mg
Total Fat	13.7 g	Cholesterol	243 mg
		Saturated Fat	5.9 g

Chef Michael Menge
The Gazebo Restaurant, New Orleans, La.

Fried Green Tomatoes

BATTER

1 egg

1/2 cup evaporated milk

1/4 teaspoon salt

1/4 teaspoon pepper

1/2 cup water

♦

3 firm tomatoes, cut into slices 1/2-inch thick

1 cup all-purpose flour

1 cup seasoned breadcrumbs

6 cups Lou Ana Vegetable Oil for frying

2 garlic cloves, minced

1/4 cup parsley, chopped

1. Prepare batter by combining batter ingredients.
2. Dip tomatoes in flour, then in batter, then in seasoned breadcrumbs.
3. Heat oil in deep fryer to 350 degrees F.
4. Drop in breaded tomatoes and fry until they rise to the top, about five minutes.
5. Place fried tomato slices on paper towels. Sprinkle with garlic and parsley.

Yield: 12 slices
Makes 6 servings (2 slices per serving)

Each serving contains:

Calories	309	Protein	4.4 g
Carbohydrate	22.1 g	Sodium	354 mg
Total Fat	22.9 g	Cholesterol	9 mg
		Saturated Fat	6 g

Chef Austin Leslie
Chez Helene Restaurant, New Orleans

Shrimp Creole

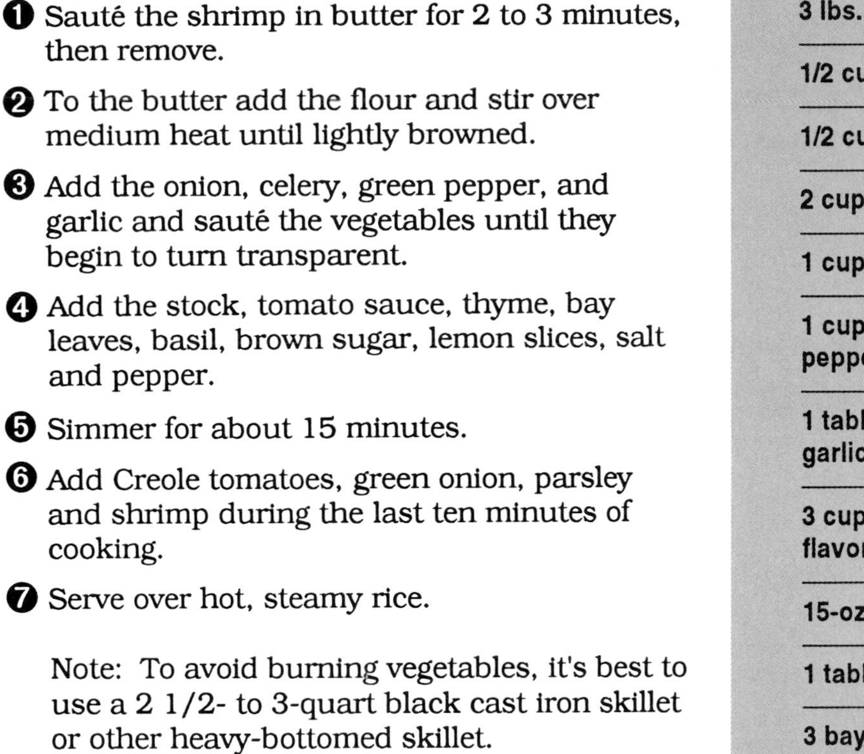

❶ Sauté the shrimp in butter for 2 to 3 minutes, then remove.

❷ To the butter add the flour and stir over medium heat until lightly browned.

❸ Add the onion, celery, green pepper, and garlic and sauté the vegetables until they begin to turn transparent.

❹ Add the stock, tomato sauce, thyme, bay leaves, basil, brown sugar, lemon slices, salt and pepper.

❺ Simmer for about 15 minutes.

❻ Add Creole tomatoes, green onion, parsley and shrimp during the last ten minutes of cooking.

❼ Serve over hot, steamy rice.

Note: To avoid burning vegetables, it's best to use a 2 1/2- to 3-quart black cast iron skillet or other heavy-bottomed skillet.

Makes 8 servings

Each serving contains:

Calories	347	Protein	35.6 g
Carbohydrate	21.2 g	Sodium	1137 mg
Total Fat	14.6 g	Cholesterol	266 mg
		Saturated Fat	7.2 g

Joe Cahn
"Keeper of the Pots & Pans"
New Orleans School of Cooking
New Orleans, La.

- 3 lbs. peeled shrimp
- 1/2 cup butter
- 1/2 cup flour
- 2 cups chopped onion
- 1 cup chopped celery
- 1 cup chopped green pepper
- 1 tablespoon chopped garlic
- 3 cups chicken stock or flavored water
- 15-oz. can tomato sauce
- 1 tablespoon thyme
- 3 bay leaves
- 1 teaspoon basil
- 1 tablespoon brown sugar
- 4 thin lemon slices
- 1/2 teaspoon salt
- 1/2 teaspoon black pepper
- 4 fresh, chopped, ripe Creole tomatoes
- 1 cup chopped green onion
- 1 cup chopped parsley

Chicken Creole

- 3 lbs. boned, skinned, chopped chicken
- 1/2 cup butter
- 1/2 cup flour
- 2 cups chopped onion
- 1 cup chopped celery
- 1 cup chopped green bell pepper
- 1 tablespoon chopped garlic
- 3 cups chicken stock or water with chicken bouillon
- 1 15-oz. can tomato sauce
- 1 tablespoon thyme
- 1 teaspoon basil
- 3 bay leaves
- 1 tablespoon brown sugar
- 4 thin lemon slices
- 1/2 teaspoon salt
- 1/2 teaspoon cayenne
- 1 cup chopped green onion
- 1 cup chopped parsley
- Cooked rice

❶ Sauté chicken in butter for two to three minutes; remove chicken from pot.

❷ To the butter add the flour and stir over medium heat until lightly browned.

❸ Add the onion, celery, green bell pepper and garlic and sauté until vegetables begin to turn transparent.

❹ Add the stock, tomato sauce, thyme, basil, bay leaves, brown sugar, lemon slices, salt and cayenne pepper. Simmer for about 15 minutes

❺ Add green onion, parsley and chicken the last five minutes of cooking.

❻ Serve over rice.

Note: To avoid burning vegetables, it's best to use a 2 1/2- to 3-quart black cast iron skillet or other heavy-bottomed skillet.

Serves eight

Each serving contains:

Calories	392	Protein	39.7 g
Carbohydrate	18.8 g	Sodium	1011 mg
Total Fat	17.4 g	Cholesterol	150 mg
		Saturated Fat	8.6 g

Joe Cahn,
"Keeper of the Pots & Pans"
New Orleans School of Cooking
New Orleans, La.

Smothered Okra & Tomatoes

- 1/3 cup of bacon drippings (from frying 1/2 lb. of bacon)
- 1/2 cup Lou Ana Vegetable Oil
- 1/2 pound ham, diced
- 1/2 pound smoked sausage, sliced 1/4-inch thick
- 2 pounds fresh okra, sliced crosswise to 1/2-inch thickness
- 1 large green bell pepper, chopped fine
- 1 large onion, chopped fine
- 1 tablespoon finely chopped garlic
- 4 large tomatoes, peeled, seeded and diced
- 1/2 pound small, peeled, raw shrimp
- 1/2 teaspoon salt
- 1/4 teaspoon black pepper
- 1/4 teaspoon cayenne pepper
- 1 teaspoon thyme
- 1 bay leaf

❶ In a large, heavy skillet (2 1/2- to 3-quart size), heat the bacon drippings and vegetable oil at a moderate heat.

❷ Add the ham and smoked sausage; brown, and then remove from the skillet; set aside.

❸ Add the okra, green bell pepper, onion and garlic, and sauté.

❹ Cover and cook until the okra is no longer slimy.

❺ Add the tomatoes, shrimp, salt, peppers, thyme and bay leaf, then the ham and sausage. Add water if needed.

❻ Cook 10 to 15 minutes on medium heat.

Makes 12 servings

Each serving contains:

Calories	301	Protein	14.8 g
Carbohydrate	10.8 g	Sodium	693 mg
Total Fat	22.2 g	Cholesterol	55 mg
		Saturated Fat	7.1 g

Chef Austin Leslie
Chez Helene Restaurant, New Orleans

The Day of the Rabbit

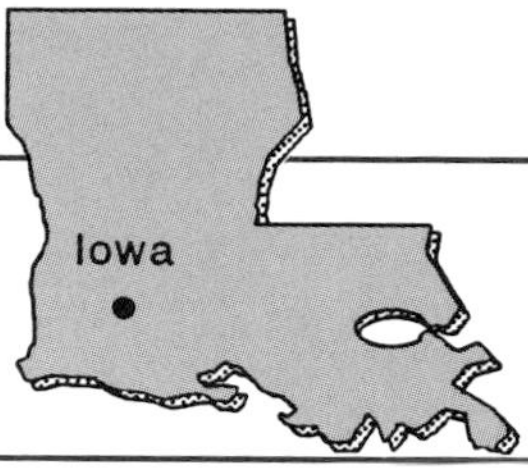

Iowa

For a town like Iowa, which is located in Cajun country, where the crawfish is king, to have a festival in honor of the rabbit seems a bit odd.

But, such a festival made good dollars and cents to organizers who put on the first Rabbit Festival in 1985. Plus, it was a lot of fun for everyone in this town 10 miles east of Lake Charles.

The festival was a natural choice after a rabbit-processing plant was built outside of Iowa. Members of the growing rabbit industry and community leaders agreed that a festival would be a good way to promote Iowa's newest enterprise and educate the public about rabbits.

The two-day event is held on the third weekend in March, which is usually before Easter, when rabbits are especially popular.

Indeed, at the Rabbit Festival, there are lots of rabbits. The local 4-H club sets up an area where rabbits are available to play with or buy.

The American Rabbit Breeder's Association brings to town Angoras, with their long, soft fur; chinchillas; the rare Flemish Giants; and the common California White.

But, many people are not aware that rabbits are good to eat, too, points out Maxine Guthery, president of the festival's board of directors.

The meat is low in fat, with a taste and texture similar to chicken. Rabbit in many guises is available to eat at the festival, and a cooking contest with rabbit as the chief ingredient is very popular. Competitors have proven they can be very inventive.

By the way, the town's name, Iowa, came from the mother state of the people who settled this town in south Louisiana.

Smothered Rabbit In Onion Gravy

- 1 rabbit, 2 1/2 to 3 pounds
- 1 1/2 teaspoons salt
- 2 teaspoons black pepper
- 1 cup all-purpose flour
- 1/4 cup Lou Ana Vegetable Oil
- 2 cups chopped onion
- 1/2 cup chopped celery
- 1/2 cup chopped green bell pepper
- 1/2 cup chopped green onion
- 2 cups water

1. Season rabbit thoroughly with salt and pepper.
2. Coat well in flour.
3. In a sauté pan, cook meat well in Lou Ana Vegetable Oil until golden brown. Remove meat from pan.
4. Add the onion, celery, green bell pepper, and green onion and sauté approximately 10 minutes. Add meat.
5. Add water.
6. Cover and simmer approximately 1 1/2 hours until tender.

Yield: 1 rabbit and 2 cups of gravy
Makes 6 servings (rabbit and gravy)

Each serving contains:

Calories	322	Protein	21.1 g
Carbohydrate	23 g	Sodium	620 mg
Total Fat	15.7 g	Cholesterol	55 mg
		Saturated Fat	4.9 g

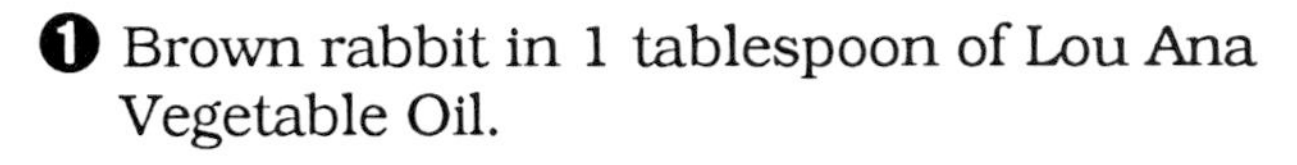

Rabbit In Red Wine

- 1 rabbit, approximately 1 pound 11 ounces
- 3 tablespoons Lou Ana Vegetable Oil, divided
- 2 tablespoons all-purpose flour
- 1 cup water
- 1 garlic clove, minced
- 1/2 teaspoon salt
- 1/2 teaspoon pepper
- 1 bay leaf
- 1 cup red cooking wine
- 1 teaspoon seasoned salt

1. Brown rabbit in 1 tablespoon of Lou Ana Vegetable Oil.
2. Remove from skillet. Drain liquid from pan.
3. Add 2 tablespoons of Lou Ana Vegetable Oil.
4. Stir in flour.
5. Add water and cook until slightly thick.
6. Add garlic, salt, pepper, bay leaf, red wine, and seasoned salt. Stir.
7. Place rabbit in sauce.
8. Cover tightly and cook until rabbit is tender.
9. Serve over steamed rice.

Makes 6 servings (not including rice)

Each serving contains:

Calories	246	Protein	19.9 g
Carbohydrate	3.4 g	Sodium	376 mg
Total Fat	13.6 g	Cholesterol	60 mg
		Saturated Fat	4.4 g

The Corniest Festival of Them All!

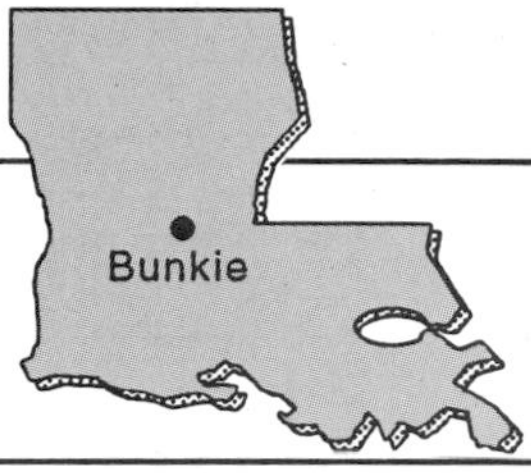

Bunkie

The Louisiana Corn Festival was created in 1987 by the Bunkie Chamber of Commerce as a way to promote the city and to honor the impact of agriculture on this central Louisiana town.

The entire community gets into the festival spirit beginning on Friday afternoon of the second full weekend in June. Merchants are judged on scarecrows they make to depict their type of business, and awards are given to the best in the bunch. Prizes are also handed out for the best residential decorations.

Children enjoy making "CORNAnimals," participating in lizard races, or entering corn-cooking, -shucking or -eating contests. The "Children's CORNer" provides sand boxes, drawing materials, games and contests for youngsters while parents take a break in the shade.

Live bands and entertainment are provided at no charge throughout the weekend.

There are fun runs, tennis, volleyball or softball tournaments to compete in, as well as pirogue races on the bayou and closest-to-the-hole events for golfers.

Adults can vie for honors in the corn-shucking or corn-eating contests.

Vendors sell everything from hot tamales to boiled fresh corn. Tasters' tickets are available to a lively cooking contest where past winners have included fresh corn and crab chowder and luscious corn desserts.

Proceeds from this family-oriented celebration are poured back into the festival.

Corn Chowder

- 2 cups whole-kernel corn
- 2 cups chopped onion
- 2 cups chopped green bell pepper
- 6 tablespoons butter, divided
- 1/4 cup all-purpose flour
- 1 quart milk
- 1 1/2 teaspoons salt
- 1/2 teaspoon pepper
- 1 cup heavy cream
- Crabmeat (optional)

1. Sauté corn, onion, and green bell pepper in 4 tablespoons of butter for 5 minutes.
2. Sprinkle with the flour and mix well.
3. Slowly add milk. Cook until thickened.
4. Simmer 20 minutes.
5. Add salt and pepper.
6. Add 1 cup of cream and 2 tablespoons of butter just before serving.
7. Optional: Add crabmeat to the bottom of the bowl when serving.

Makes 8 servings

Each serving contains:

Calories	341	Protein	7.2 g
Carbohydrate	25.4 g	Sodium	701 mg
Total Fat	24.9 g	Cholesterol	82 mg
		Saturated Fat	15 g

Real Corn Oysters

- 1 cup cornmeal
- 1 cup all-purpose flour
- 2 teaspoons baking powder
- 1/2 teaspoon pepper
- 1/2 teaspoon salt
- 1/2 cup 2% low-fat milk
- 2 eggs, separated
- 1 cup finely chopped oysters
- 2 cups Lou Ana Vegetable Oil

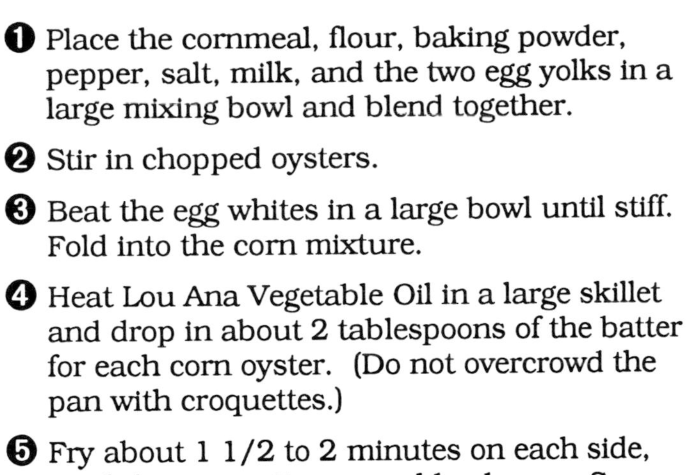

1. Place the cornmeal, flour, baking powder, pepper, salt, milk, and the two egg yolks in a large mixing bowl and blend together.
2. Stir in chopped oysters.
3. Beat the egg whites in a large bowl until stiff. Fold into the corn mixture.
4. Heat Lou Ana Vegetable Oil in a large skillet and drop in about 2 tablespoons of the batter for each corn oyster. (Do not overcrowd the pan with croquettes.)
5. Fry about 1 1/2 to 2 minutes on each side, until the croquettes are golden brown. Serve hot.

Preparation time: 5 minutes. Cooking time: 3 to 4 minutes.

Yield: 6 to 8 servings (32 croquettes)

Each croquette contains:

Calories	57	Protein	1.2 g
Carbohydrate	4.7 g	Sodium	39 mg
Total Fat	3.6 g	Cholesterol	15 mg
		Saturated Fat	1 g

Chicken Ro-Tel

1 pound chicken, cooked and deboned

1 package (7 oz.) vermicelli, cooked in broth

1/2 cup water

2 cups chopped onion

2 large green bell peppers, chopped

1/4 cup butter, melted

1 can (10 ounces) tomatoes with chilies

1 can (8 ounces) mushrooms, drained

1 can (16 ounces) whole-kernel corn, drained

2 tablespoons Worcestershire sauce

1 pound processed cheese spread

❶ In a stock pot, cook chicken until tender. Debone, chop, and set aside.

❷ Cook vermicelli in chicken broth. Add water, if necessary, to have adequate liquid for cooking. Cook until tender and drain well.

❸ Sauté onion and green bell peppers in melted butter. Remove from heat.

❹ Add tomatoes, mushrooms, corn, Worcestershire sauce, and cheese to the onion mixture.

❺ Mix sauce with vermicelli and chopped chicken.

❻ Pour mixture into a 9" x 13" x 2 1/2" pan. (If desired, 1/2 cup of broth can be added to produce a more juicy final product.)

❼ Bake at 350 degrees F. for approximately 30 minutes.

Yield: 11 cups
Makes 10 servings

Each serving contains:

Calories	365	Protein	22.7 g
Carbohydrate	28.5 g	Sodium	1191 mg
Total Fat	16.9 g	Cholesterol	83 mg
		Saturated Fat	9.9 g

From "Aw Shucks Recipes,"
official recipe book of the Louisiana Corn Festival

Corn Casserole Supreme

1/4 cup all-purpose flour

2 tablespoons sugar

3 eggs, beaten

4 cups whole-kernel corn

2 cups shredded sharp cheese

10 slices of bacon, cooked and crumbled

1/2 teaspoon salt

1. Preheat oven to 350 degrees F.
2. Combine flour and sugar in a 2-quart bowl.
3. Add beaten eggs and mix well.
4. Stir in corn, shredded cheese, crumbled bacon, and salt.
5. Pour mixture in 6" x 10" x 1 1/2" baking dish.
6. Bake for 30 minutes or until set.

Yield: 4 cups
Makes 8 servings (1/2 cup each)

Each serving contains:

Calories	270	Protein	13.9 g
Carbohydrate	20 g	Sodium	695 mg
Total Fat	15.7 g	Cholesterol	139 mg
		Saturated Fat	8 g

From "Aw Shucks Recipes,"
official recipe book of the Louisiana Corn Festival

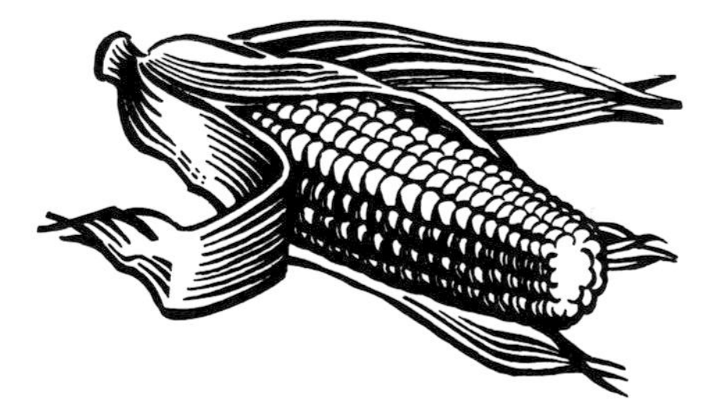

Mexican Sour Cream Enchiladas

- 1/2 cup chopped onion
- 1 can (4 ounces) mushrooms
- 1 clove garlic
- 2 tablespoons butter
- 1 3/4 cups cooked chicken
- 1 can (4 ounces) green chilies
- 3 cups sour cream, divided
- 1 1/2 tablespoons chili powder
- 1 teaspoon ground cumin
- 1 teaspoon salt
- 1/4 teaspoon pepper
- Lou Ana Corn Oil
- 18 corn tortillas
- 4 cups shredded cheddar cheese
- 1 can (14 ounces) tomatoes
- 1 can (10 ounces) tomatoes with chilies

1. Sauté onion, mushrooms, and garlic in butter until tender, but do not brown. Add cooked chicken, chilies, 1 cup of sour cream, chili powder, cumin, salt and pepper.
2. Heat over low heat, stirring frequently, only until hot. Remove from heat.
3. Meanwhile, pour Lou Ana Corn Oil into 8" skillet, filling about 1/2" deep.* Fry tortillas, one at a time, in hot oil until soft (3 to 5 seconds). Drain on paper towels.
4. Spread a heaping tablespoon of filling in center of each tortilla. Sprinkle with cheddar cheese. Fold sides over filling. Place seam side down in greased 13" x 9" x 2" baking dish. Repeat procedure for all tortillas.
5. Mix canned tomatoes and canned tomatoes with chilies. Pour over enchiladas.
6. Bake at 350 degrees F. for 15 minutes.
7. Spread remaining 2 cups of sour cream and remaining cheese over top of enchiladas. Bake 8 minutes. Don't overbake during last step, or sour cream will curdle.

* Microwave oven can be used to heat and soften tortillas, eliminating the frying step.

Yield: 18 enchiladas
Makes 9 servings (2 enchiladas per person)

*Each enchilada has:***
Calories 288
Carbohydrate ...... 15.6 g
Total Fat .... 19.1 g
Protein .... 14.4 g
Sodium .... 354 mg
Cholesterol .... 66 mg
Saturated Fat ..... 11.7 g

** Using microwave method.

From "Aw Shucks Recipes," official recipe book of the Louisiana Corn Festival

Meatballs Con Queso

- 1 1/2 pounds ground chuck
- 1 1/2 cups breadcrumbs
- 1/3 cup minced onion
- 1/3 cup milk
- 1/3 cup chopped parsley
- 1/4 teaspoon black pepper
- 1/8 teaspoon Tabasco sauce
- 1 egg
- 1/4 cup Lou Ana Corn Oil, for frying
- 1 can (4 ounces) green chili peppers, chopped
- 1 package (1 1/4 oz.) taco seasoning mix
- 3/4 cup water
- 1 pound cheddar cheese
- Cooked cornbread

1. Mix ground chuck, breadcrumbs, onion, milk, parsley, black pepper, Tabasco sauce and egg in large bowl.
2. Shape into small meatballs.
3. Fry each in preheated Lou Ana Corn Oil until meatballs are brown.
4. Remove and drain on absorbent paper.
5. In a large skillet add chilies with their juice, taco seasoning mix and water.
6. Heat until the mixture boils.
7. Place the meatballs in the skillet and simmer until the meatballs are heated through, stirring carefully.
8. Stir in cheese and remove from heat.
9. Serve in a chafing dish.
10. Serve with cornbread.

May be served as a main dish or appetizer.

Yield: 48 meatballs
Makes 8 servings (6 meatballs per serving)

Each serving contains:

Calories	551	Protein	33.3 g
Carbohydrate	19.3 g	Sodium	670 mg
Total Fat	37.3 g	Cholesterol	153 mg
		Saturated Fat	19.5 g

Cornmeal Flapjacks

- 1 cup all-purpose flour
- 1 cup cornmeal
- 1 teaspoon salt
- 2 tablespoons sugar
- 1 1/8 cups boiling water
- 2 eggs, separated
- 1 tablespoon Lou Ana Vegetable Oil, to grease griddle

1. Mix flour, cornmeal, salt, and sugar in a one-quart bowl.
2. Add boiling water. Stir until all dry ingredients are thoroughly moistened. Cool.
3. Add egg yolks to cooled batter. Mix well.
4. Beat egg whites until stiff. Fold into batter. (Thin batter with additional water if needed.)
5. Lightly grease a griddle and heat.
6. On preheated griddle, pour 1/4 cup of batter for each griddle cake. When brown, turn and brown other side.
7. Serve immediately with butter and syrup.

Makes 12 flapjacks

Each flapjack contains:
Calories 112
Carbohydrate ...... 19.1 g
Total Fat .... 2.4 g
Protein .... 3.1 g
Sodium .... 206 mg
Cholesterol .... 46 mg
Saturated Fat .... 0.6 g

From "Aw Shucks Recipes," official recipe book of the Louisiana Corn Festival

Country Cornbread

❶ Preheat oven to 425 degrees F.

❷ Use Lou Ana Corn Oil to grease nine muffin cups.

❸ In a one-quart bowl, sift together cornmeal, flour, salt, and baking powder. Stir well.

❹ In a small bowl beat together egg and milk, mixing well. Add to dry ingredients.

❺ Fill muffin cups 1/2 to 2/3 full.

❻ Bake for 15 to 20 minutes in preheated oven.

Yield: 9 muffins

Each muffin contains:
Calories 146
Carbohydrate .... 24 g
Total Fat .... 3.5 g
Protein .... 4.3 g
Sodium .... 336 mg
Cholesterol .... 35 mg
Saturated Fat .... 1.2 g

From "Aw Shucks Recipes," official recipe book of the Louisiana Corn Festival

1 tablespoon Lou Ana Corn Oil

1 cup cornmeal

1/2 cup all-purpose flour

1 teaspoon salt

1 tablespoon baking powder

1 egg

1 cup milk

TONY O. CHAMPAGNE

Winnsboro

Love That Fried Catfish!

When it's done right, there is nothing in the world quite like farm-raised catfish, dipped in cornmeal and fried to a golden brown.

This Louisiana delicacy is the main attraction at the Catfish Festival, held in Winnsboro annually on the second Saturday in April.

The festival began in 1987 when a group of local citizens decided to highlight the growing aquaculture industry in the Winnsboro area. Catfish farms with thousands of acres of ponds were popping up throughout the parish. There was one processing plant to service them and a second plant and feed mill were in the planning stages. This new industry spawned a festival that promoted both Franklin Parish and catfish.

The first festival was designed as a family day with music, a petting zoo, food booths, a 5-K run, photo contest, cooking contest and more. The attendance at the first festival exceeded the modest predictions that were made, and in four years the crowds grew to approximately 40,000.

The festival today offers a wide variety of music, from bluegrass to symphony brass quintets to local high school bands. Special attractions have included the Wallendas' high wire act, Civil War re-enactments, softball tournaments, clogging, antique car exhibits and visits by local celebrities.

Catfish is the reason for the festival, of course, and eating catfish is the main event. The LSU Cooperative Extension Service organizes townspeople to cook mounds of meal-fried catfish to serve with cole slaw and hush puppies during the festival. As much as 5,000 pounds of catfish have been consumed at one festival.

Catfish & Eggs

- 5 tablespoons butter, to be divided
- 1/2 cup chopped green onion
- 1/2 cup chopped celery
- 1/2 cup chopped green bell pepper
- 12 eggs, beaten
- 1 pound farm-raised catfish, cooked and flaked
- 6 1/2 ounces cooked shrimp
- 1 cup canned mushrooms
- 2 tablespoons all-purpose flour
- 1 1/4 cups half-and-half cream
- 4 teaspoons hot sauce
- 1 cup 100% natural shredded mozzarella cheese
- 1/4 cup grated Parmesan cheese
- 3 tablespoons dry white wine

1. Preheat oven to 350 degrees F.
2. Lightly grease a 2 1/2-quart baking dish.
3. In a large skillet, melt three tablespoons of butter; sauté green onion, celery, and green bell pepper in butter until tender.
4. Add eggs; stir until eggs are set. (They should have appearance of scrambled eggs.)
5. Remove from heat and fold in catfish, shrimp, and mushrooms. Set mixture aside.
6. In medium sauce pan, melt two tablespoons of butter.
7. Stir in flour; add half-and-half and hot sauce. Cook until mixture thickens, stirring constantly.
8. Add mozzarella cheese, Parmesan cheese and wine.
9. Stir until smooth.
10. Fold sauce into scrambled egg mixture.
11. Pour into prepared baking dish.
12. Bake for 15 minutes.

TOPPING

1 can (8 ounces) refrigerated Quick Crescent Dinner Rolls

1 tablespoon melted butter

1 tablespoon chopped parsley

1. Remove dough from can in rolled sections; do not unroll.
2. Cut the roll into twelve slices; cut each slice in half.
3. Arrange 20 half-slices flat edge down around the edges of the baking dish containing the egg and fish.
4. Arrange remaining four slices in center of the mixture.
5. Combine one tablespoon melted butter and parsley; brush lightly over dough surfaces.
6. Return and bake at 375 degrees F. until dough is golden brown.
7. Let stand for five minutes before serving.
8. Garnish as desired.

Yield: 8 cups
Makes 12 servings (2/3 cup each)

Each serving contains:

Calories	384	Protein	25.6 g
Carbohydrate	11.8 g	Sodium	500 mg
Total Fat	25.9 g	Cholesterol	361 mg
		Saturated Fat	8.5 g

Leanna Walters
First Place, Main Dishes, Youth Division, 1988

Catfish Gumbo

- 1 pound catfish fillets
- 1/2 cup chopped celery
- 1/2 cup chopped green bell pepper
- 1/2 cup chopped onion
- 1 clove garlic, chopped
- 1/4 cup Lou Ana Vegetable Oil
- 2 beef bouillon cubes
- 2 cups boiling water
- 1 can (16 ounces) tomatoes
- 1 package (10 ounces) frozen okra
- 1 teaspoon salt
- 1/4 teaspoon red pepper
- 1/4 teaspoon thyme
- 1 whole bay leaf
- 1/8 teaspoon Tabasco sauce
- 1 1/2 cups cooked rice

1. Cut fillets into one-inch pieces. Set aside.
2. Cook celery, green pepper, onion, and garlic in oil until tender.
3. In a 3- or 4-quart saucepot, dissolve bouillon cubes in boiling water.
4. Add tomatoes, okra, seasonings and sautéed vegetables to the bouillon.
5. Cover and simmer for 30 minutes.
6. Add fish.
7. Cover and simmer for 15 minutes, or until the fish flakes easily when tested with a fork.
8. Remove bay leaf.
9. Place 1/4 cup of rice in each of six soup bowls and fill with gumbo.

Yield: 7 cups of gumbo (without rice)
Makes 6 servings of gumbo with rice

Each serving contains:
Calories 287
Carbohydrate .... 20 g
Total Fat .... 16.9 g
Protein .... 14.3 g
Sodium .... 720 mg
Cholesterol .... 25 mg
Saturated Fat .... 2.3 g

Lorraine Ensminger
Second Place, 1988

Catfish Crab Rolls

- 6 small (2 pounds) fish fillets, skinned
- 1/4 cup melted butter, divided
- 1 cup unseasoned croutons
- 2 tablespoons chopped parsley
- 1 jar (2 ounces) minced pimientos
- 2 green onions, chopped
- 1 beaten egg
- 1 can (6 ounces) crabmeat, cooked
- 1 teaspoon seasoned salt
- 1 can (4 ounces) mushrooms, drained
- 1 package (10 ounces) immature frozen English peas, cooked
- 1/2 teaspoon paprika

1. Preheat oven to 375 degrees F.
2. Wash and dry fillets.
3. Melt butter and mix with croutons, parsley, pimientos, onion, egg, and crabmeat.
4. Season with seasoned salt.
5. Spoon filling onto fillets and coil from small end.
6. Secure with toothpicks.
7. Place fillets in greased baking dish and spoon some of the melted butter over top.
8. Bake in oven for 20 minutes or until fish flakes.
9. Remove from oven.
10. Arrange mushrooms and peas around the fish rolls and garnish with paprika.
11. Serve with cream sauce, if desired.

Makes 6 servings

Each serving contains:

Calories	410	Protein	32.7 g
Carbohydrate	15.5 g	Sodium	771 mg
Total Fat	24.4 g	Cholesterol	145 mg
		Saturated Fat	5.2 g

Nikki Thornton
Second Place, 1988

Catfish Parmesan

- 2 pounds catfish fillets (4 to 6 fillets)
- 1 cup sour cream
- 1/4 cup Parmesan cheese
- 1 tablespoon lemon juice
- 1 tablespoon grated onion
- 1/2 teaspoon salt
- 1/4 teaspoon red pepper
- 1/4 teaspoon paprika

1. Preheat oven to 350 degrees F.
2. Place catfish fillets in a single layer on the bottom of a well-greased 12" x 8" x 2" baking dish.
3. Combine remaining ingredients except paprika.
4. Spread mixture over fish.
5. Sprinkle with paprika.
6. Bake for 25 to 30 minutes or until fish flakes easily.
7. If desired, garnish with parsley sprigs.

Yield: 6 servings

Each serving contains:

Calories	321	Protein	25.4 g
Carbohydrate	2.2 g	Sodium	331 mg
Total Fat	23.7 g	Cholesterol	70 mg
		Saturated Fat	5.7 g

Mikki Bowen
First Place, Other Division, Youth Category, 1988

Catfish Franklin

 In a 12" x 7 1/2" x 2" glass baking dish, combine all ingredients except fish, shrimp, and wine.

2. Micro-cook covered with waxed paper on 100 percent power (high), for five to six minutes, stirring twice.

3. Stir in shrimp and wine.

4. Place fish fillets atop mixture, folding any thin edges under; spoon some sauce over fillets.

5. Cook on high five to seven minutes, or until fish flakes.

Makes 6 servings

Each serving contains:			
Calories	236	Protein	21 g
Carbohydrate	3.5 g	Sodium	338 mg
Total Fat	15 g	Cholesterol	74 mg
		Saturated Fat	2.4 g

Katherine Bowen
First Place, Adult Division

1/2 cup Rotel tomatoes with chilies

1/2 cup chopped onion

1/2 cup chopped green bell pepper

1 can (4 ounces) mushrooms

2 tablespoons butter

2 tablespoons lemon juice

1 tablespoon chopped parsley

1/2 teaspoon thyme

1/4 teaspoon salt

1 can (4 1/2 ounces) shrimp

1/4 cup white wine

1 1/2 pounds catfish fillets

TONY O. CHAMPAGNE

Even Presidents Hunt Ducks Near Gueydan

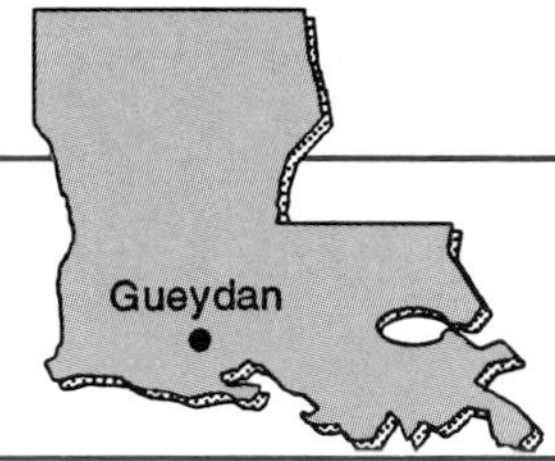

Gueydan

Gueydan, where the land begins to turn to marsh at the edge of the Gulf of Mexico, is the Duck Capital of America and home of the Gueydan Duck Festival.

The festival, held the second weekend in November to coincide with the opening of duck hunting season, shows just how important the fowl is to this small community.

Camouflage hunting clothes are the outfit of choice for this event, and the sound of duck calls fills the air. A popular event at this festival is a duck call competition where contestants of all ages and both sexes reproduce their most convincing calls.

The festival began in 1976 and is run today by the Duck Festival Association. Festivities are held on a 12-acre site donated to the Vermilion Parish Police Jury by Atlantic Richfield Company for use by the festival association.

Festival organizers boast of a schedule that includes a parade, Duck Dash (one mile and 5K races), carnival, arts and crafts and cooking contests. The winning duck and wildlife recipes are featured in a festival cookbook (updated annually) which can be purchased during the festival.

Well-trained dogs are an important part of duck hunting, and the American Kennel Club's local chapter sponsors dog trials during the festival.

Gueydan has "the best duck hunting in the nation," says one festival organizer. More than just a few celebrities, including U.S. presidents, have made the trek to Gueydan for a hunt.

'Fully Packed Quack' (Baked Stuffed Duck)

- 1 pound ground round (beef)
- 1 pound ground sausage, regular
- 1 cup chopped onion
- 1 cup chopped green bell pepper
- 1 can (4 ounces) mushrooms, stems and pieces
- 1 can (8 ounces) chopped water chestnuts
- 1 cup chopped parsley
- 1 can (10 3/4 ounces) cream of chicken soup
- 1 pound American cheese, cubed
- 4 cups cooked rice
- 1 cup seasoned dry breadcrumbs
- 1 duck (approximately 4 pounds)
- 1/4 teaspoon red pepper
- 1/4 teaspoon black pepper
- 1/2 teaspoon garlic salt

1. Brown ground round and sausage. Drain.
2. Add onion and green bell pepper and cook until tender.
3. Add mushrooms, water chestnuts, parsley, and soup. Heat thoroughly.
4. Add cheese and cook over a low heat until cheese melts.
5. Stir in rice and breadcrumbs. Set aside.
6. Preheat oven to 350 degrees F.
7. Stuff duck with part of stuffing. Reserve remaining stuffing to serve with duck.
8. Season duck with red pepper, black pepper and garlic salt.
9. Place stuffed duck on roasting rack that has been placed in a shallow baking pan.
10. Cook in preheated oven until tender, about 2 1/2 hours.

Yield: 1 duck and 11 cups of stuffing
Makes 10 servings

Each serving contains:

Calories	621	Protein	40.6 g
Carbohydrate	33.6 g	Sodium	1595 mg
Total Fat	34.9 g	Cholesterol	139 mg
		Saturated Fat	16.8 g

Ariana Hanks
Junior Division, 1988

Duck With Turnips

1. Mix chopped vegetables for stuffing.
2. Stuff duck with part of vegetable stuffing. Set aside remainder of stuffing.
3. Season duck with salt, black pepper, and red pepper.
4. Place stuffed duck in Dutch oven. Add 2 cups of water, cover Dutch oven and place over medium heat.
5. Simmer for two hours or until tender. Add more water as needed to prevent burning.
6. During last 20 minutes, add remaining vegetable stuffing to Dutch oven and cook until tender.

Yield: 2 cups of vegetables plus 1 duck
Makes 6 servings

Each serving contains:

Calories	144	Protein	14.6 g
Carbohydrate	6 g	Sodium	277 mg
Total Fat	6.7 g	Cholesterol	52 mg
		Saturated Fat	2.5 g

Kimberly Mouton

2 cups chopped turnip

1/2 cup chopped onion

1/2 cup chopped green bell pepper

1/2 cup chopped celery

1/2 cup chopped carrot

1 duck (approximately 4 1/4 pounds)

1/2 teaspoon salt

1/2 teaspoon black pepper

1/4 teaspoon red pepper

2 cups water

Baked Duck

- 1 duck (approximately 4 pounds)
- 1/4 cup chopped celery
- 1/2 cup chopped green onion bottoms
- 1/2 cup chopped green bell pepper
- 1/4 cup chopped green onion tops
- 3 tablespoons butter

1. Preheat oven to 350 degrees F.
2. Stuff duck with celery, green onion bottoms, green bell pepper, and onion tops.
3. Slit breast on both sides and put half of the butter in the slit on one side and the other half of the butter in the slit on the other.
4. Bake for 2 to 2 1/2 hours.

Yield: 1 baked duck
Makes 8 servings

Each serving contains:

Calories	117	Protein	8.6 g
Carbohydrate	1.7 g	Sodium	72 mg
Total Fat	8.4 g	Cholesterol	44 mg
		Saturated Fat	4.2 g

Jennifer Lemaire
First Place, Senior Division, 1988

Duck With Rice Dressing

- 1 duck (approximately 4 pounds)
- 2 teaspoons seasoned salt, to be divided
- 2 tablespoons all-purpose flour
- 2 tablespoons Lou Ana Vegetable Oil
- 1/2 pound ground chuck
- 1/2 cup chopped celery
- 1/2 cup chopped green bell pepper
- 1/2 cup chopped onion
- 1 cup water
- 1/2 cup chopped parsley
- 1/2 cup chopped green onion tops
- 3/4 teaspoon salt
- 1/2 teaspoon black pepper
- 4 cups cooked rice

DUCK

1. Preheat oven to 350 degrees F.
2. Rub 1 teaspoon of seasoned salt into duck.
3. Bake in oven until duck is tender and golden brown (2 to 2 1/2 hours).
4. While duck is baking, prepare dressing.

DRESSING

1. Prepare brown roux with flour and oil.
2. Stir in beef, celery, green bell pepper, and onion.
3. Add water and simmer until done.
4. Add parsley, green onion tops, salt, pepper, and remaining teaspoon of seasoned salt.
5. Add rice and mix well.

Yield: 1 duck and 7 1/2 cups of stuffing
Makes 8 servings

Each serving contains:

Calories	287	Protein	19.6 g
Carbohydrate	27.6 g	Sodium	862 mg
Total Fat	10.3 g	Cholesterol	55 mg
		Saturated Fat	3.2 g

Susan M. Lougon
Senior Division, 1988

Italian Zucchini Pie

- 4 cups thinly sliced zucchini
- 1 cup chopped onion
- 1/2 cup canned mushrooms
- 1/2 cup butter
- 1/2 pound cooked shrimp
- 1/2 cup chopped parsley
- 1/2 teaspoon salt
- 1/2 teaspoon pepper
- 1/2 teaspoon garlic powder
- 1/4 teaspoon basil
- 1/4 teaspoon oregano
- 2 eggs, beaten
- 8 ounces shredded mozzarella cheese
- 1 can (8 ounces) crescent dinner rolls
- 1 tablespoon prepared mustard

1. Preheat oven to 375 degrees F.
2. Sauté zucchini, onion, and mushrooms in butter 10 minutes.
3. Stir in shrimp, seasonings, eggs, and cheese. Remove from heat. Set aside.
4. Separate crescent roll dough. Place pieces of dough in bottom of an ungreased 10-inch pie plate and press into bottom and up the sides of the pie plate to form a crust.
5. Spread the prepared mustard over the crust.
6. Pour vegetable mixture into the crust.
7. Bake for 18 to 20 minutes.
8. Cover edges of crust with foil during last minutes of baking, if necessary, to prevent excessive browning.
9. Let stand 10 minutes.
10. Cut and serve.

Yield: 10 slices
Makes 10 servings

Each serving contains:

Calories	286	Protein	17 g
Carbohydrate	12.2 g	Sodium	619 mg
Total Fat	19.3 g	Cholesterol	146 mg
		Saturated Fat	8.5 g

Lynette Trahan
First Place, 1988

Super Chocolate Nut Cookies

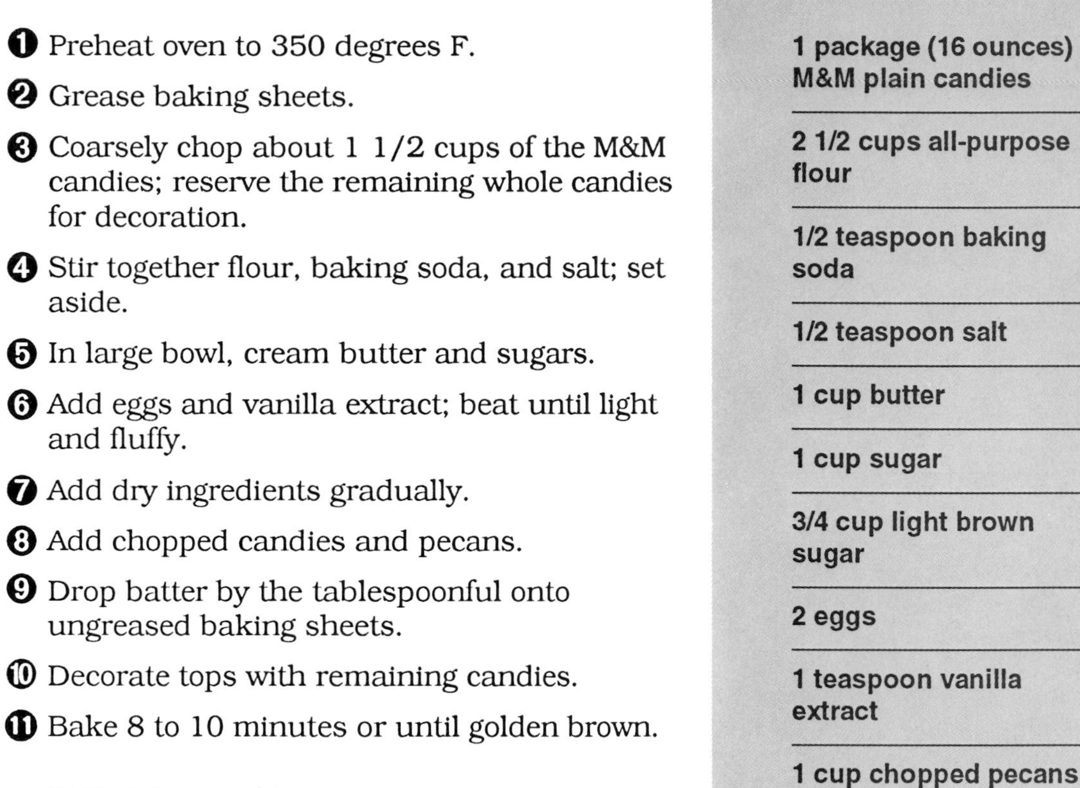

1 package (16 ounces) M&M plain candies

2 1/2 cups all-purpose flour

1/2 teaspoon baking soda

1/2 teaspoon salt

1 cup butter

1 cup sugar

3/4 cup light brown sugar

2 eggs

1 teaspoon vanilla extract

1 cup chopped pecans

1. Preheat oven to 350 degrees F.
2. Grease baking sheets.
3. Coarsely chop about 1 1/2 cups of the M&M candies; reserve the remaining whole candies for decoration.
4. Stir together flour, baking soda, and salt; set aside.
5. In large bowl, cream butter and sugars.
6. Add eggs and vanilla extract; beat until light and fluffy.
7. Add dry ingredients gradually.
8. Add chopped candies and pecans.
9. Drop batter by the tablespoonful onto ungreased baking sheets.
10. Decorate tops with remaining candies.
11. Bake 8 to 10 minutes or until golden brown.

Yield: 7 dozen cookies

Each cookie contains:

Calories	89	Protein	1 g
Carbohydrate	12.2 g	Sodium	49 mg
Total Fat	4.3 g	Cholesterol	13 mg
		Saturated Fat	2.1 g

Mandy Stelly
First Place, 1988

tony a. CHAMPAGNE

Fried Alligator, Anyone?

Franklin

"If the thought of eating alligator turns you off, your mind is causing your mouth to miss out on some delicious eating," says Margie Luke, author of "The Gourmet Gator" and promoter of the annual International Alligator Festival.

The day-long October festival in Franklin features an alligator-cooking contest as highly competitive as it is mouth-watering. In fact, the idea of such a cookoff is what gave birth to the festival.

In 1981 a harvest festival was planned as a fund-raiser for the local parochial schools. That was also the year the State Department of Wildlife and Fisheries established an alligator season in Louisiana. At the last minute an alligator-cooking contest was added to the festival.

About a dozen cooks entered that first year, and the competition proved so popular that the festival was changed to the International Alligator Festival.

The white meat in the alligator tail is considered by some to be the most delicious cut. It has the texture and taste of fish, while the meat on the legs is pink and looks like chicken.

Alligator, correctly prepared, can be substituted for beef, fish, poultry, pork, lamb or turtle, Mrs. Luke says. It has the advantage of having low sodium and cholesterol levels.

Festival-goers can sample fried alligator and alligator sauce piquante along with more ordinary hamburgers and hot dogs.

Live music, a carnival, arts and crafts and street dances round out the day's activities. A larger dance, fondly called the "Gator Bash," is held the following week along with a silent auction.

Judge Fleming's Famous *Potage De Cocodrile A La Teche*

- 1 pound alligator meat, cut into 1-inch cubes
- 5 tablespoons Lou Ana Vegetable Oil, divided
- 3 tablespoons unsifted all-purpose flour
- 1/2 cup chopped green bell pepper
- 1 cup chopped onion
- 1/3 cup chopped celery
- 2 green onions, chopped
- 1 garlic clove, chopped
- 1 cup Rotel tomatoes with chilies
- 1/2 cup tomato sauce
- 1 bay leaf
- 2 cups water
- 3/4 cup white wine
- 1 tablespoon Worcestershire sauce
- 1/2 teaspoon salt
- 1/4 teaspoon white pepper
- 1/2 teaspoon Creole seasoning

1. Cook the cubed alligator in 2 tablespoons of oil in skillet for 15 minutes. Set aside.
2. Make a dark brown roux with the remaining 3 tablespoons of oil and the flour.
3. Add green bell pepper, onion, celery, green onion and garlic. Cook until wilted.
4. Add Rotel tomatoes, tomato sauce, bay leaf, water, wine, Worcestershire sauce, salt, white pepper and Creole seasoning. Cook slowly for 20 minutes.
5. Add cooked alligator to soup and cook slowly for 45 minutes or until alligator is tender.

Yield: Approximately 4 cups
Serves 4

Each serving contains:

Calories	515	Protein	54.1 g
Carbohydrate	15 g	Sodium	763 mg
Total Fat	22.2 g	Cholesterol	0 mg
		Saturated Fat	4.3 g

Judge Robert M. Fleming

Stuffed Eggplant With Alligator

1/3 pound ground alligator

2 tablespoons butter

1/3 cup chopped onion

1/4 cup chopped celery

1/4 cup chopped green bell pepper

1 garlic clove, minced

1 eggplant

1 teaspoon seasoned salt

1 egg, beaten

1/4 cup canned mushrooms (stems & pieces)

1/3 cup chopped onion tops

1/4 cup Italian bread-crumbs

2 tablespoons Italian breadcrumbs (to sprinkle on top)

1. Preheat oven to 375 degrees F.
2. Cook alligator meat in melted butter as you would ground beef.
3. Add onion, celery, green bell pepper, and garlic. Cook until tender.
4. Cut eggplant lengthwise and remove pulp. Place eggplant shells in water to which lemon juice has been added. The acid will retard browning.
5. Cut pulp in cubes (3/4"-1"). Add to meat mixture and cook until tender. Remove from heat.
6. Add seasoned salt, egg, mushrooms, onion tops, and breadcrumbs. Mix well.
7. Stuff meat mixture into the two eggplant shell halves. Sprinkle top with breadcrumbs.
8. Bake for 20 minutes.

Yield: 2 cups
Makes 4 servings (1/2 cup each)

Each serving contains:

Calories	218	Protein	21.2 g
Carbohydrate	12.2 g	Sodium	689 mg
Total Fat	9.2 g	Cholesterol	83 mg
		Saturated Fat	4.1 g

Paul J. Comeaux

TONY D. CHAMPAGNE

Pirates Occupy Lake Charles During Contraband Days

Lake Charles

Brandishing cutlasses, marauding pirates invade the city of Lake Charles during the annual Contraband Days festival, a family-oriented extravaganza that attracts some 300,000 visitors each May.

Contraband Days, which lasts for two weeks, derives its name from legendary pirates, such as the infamous "Gentleman Pirate," Jean Lafitte, who would retreat into the numerous bayous along Louisiana's Gulf Coast when threatened by weather or enemy ships.

Along the winding waterways, the pirates would bury their contraband for safe keeping. According to legend, sometimes they lost their way, and some of the treasure remains to be found.

Contraband Days began in 1958 as a one-day celebration, but its increasing popularity led to the creation of a non-profit festival run by local businesses. It now claims to be the second largest festival in Louisiana next to Mardi Gras in New Orleans.

The festival's 259-member board strives to provide something fun for all ages. From the boom of the pirate's cannon, to the whisper of wind on the lake, to the poignant music of the carousel, to the music of more than 40 bands from all over the United States, there is something for everyone.

Boat owners, with their vessels decorated, participate in a parade along the seawall and toss doubloons and candy to the eager crowd.

There are pet shows and bed races, but also such top name entertainment as Bob Hope and David Copperfield, previous Contraband Days performers.

The festival is held at the Lake Charles Civic Center and on 64 acres beside the lake. The celebration concludes with the Grand Fireworks Display.

Pirates Pies

- 1 pound ground round (beef)
- 1 garlic clove, chopped
- 1 cup chopped onion
- 1/2 cup chopped green bell pepper
- 1/3 cup chopped celery
- 1/3 cup chopped green onion
- 1 1/2 teaspoons salt
- 1 teaspoon black pepper
- 1 dash red pepper
- 1 cup cooked rice
- 1/2 cup catsup
- 1 tablespoon parsley flakes

- 5 1/2 cups self-rising flour
- 2/3 cup plus 2 tablespoons shortening
- 2 eggs, beaten
- 1 3/4 cups milk
- 8 cups Lou Ana Vegetable Oil for frying

FILLING

1. Combine beef, garlic, onion, bell pepper, celery, green onion, salt, black pepper, and red pepper.
2. Cook until meat is thoroughly browned.
3. Add rice, stirring until well-mixed with beef.
4. Remove from heat; cool.
5. Drain off excess fat.
6. Add catsup and parsley.
7. Mix well.

DOUGH

1. Sift flour; cut shortening into flour.
2. Mix eggs and milk together. Add to shortening/flour mixture. Stir to form a dough.
3. Form dough into a ball.
4. Roll about 1/3 of the dough at a time on a lightly floured board.
5. Cut dough in 5 1/2-inch diameter circles (or squares).

6. Place two heaping tablespoons of Filling on dough.
7. Dampen edges of dough circles. Fold over meat.
8. Crimp edges with a fork.
9. Prick with a fork on top.
10. Deep fry at 350 degrees F. until golden brown.

Yield: 26 pies
Makes 26 servings

Each pie contains:

Calories	332	Protein	7.2 g
Carbohydrate	21.6 g	Sodium	556 mg
Total Fat	23.9 g	Cholesterol	33 mg
		Saturated Fat	5.7 g

Janet L. Hoste

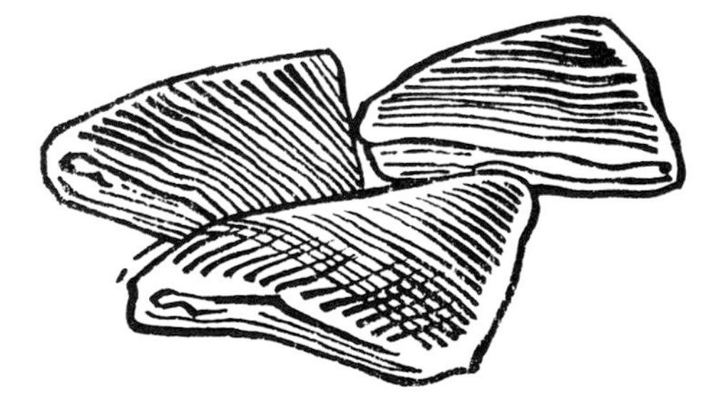

Crawfish & Rice Quiche

- 3/4 cup chopped onion
- 1 tablespoon butter
- 4 beaten eggs
- 2/3 cup Half & Half cream
- 1/2 pound cooked crawfish *
- 3/4 cup grated jalapeno cheese
- 1/2 cup chopped black olives
- 1/2 cup chopped pimiento
- 1/2 cup chopped canned mushrooms
- 1/2 cup chopped green onion tops
- 2 cups cooked rice
- 1 10-inch pastry shell, uncooked

1. Sauté the onion in butter until wilted.
2. Blend together eggs and Half & Half cream.
3. Add sautéed onion and remaining ingredients (except pastry shell) to egg/cream mixture; stir well.
4. Pour into quiche dish lined with pastry.
5. Bake 10 minutes at 450 degrees F., then bake 25 minutes longer at 325 degrees F.

*May use shrimp, if desired.

Yield: One 10-inch pie
Makes 10 servings

Each serving contains:

Calories	295	Protein	11.6 g
Carbohydrate	22.4 g	Sodium	498 mg
Total Fat	17.7 g	Cholesterol	144 mg
		Saturated Fat	6.1 g

Sharon Phenice
First Place

Rice Farmers Casserole

- 1 cup chopped green onion
- 1/4 cup chopped red bell pepper
- 1/2 cup chopped green bell pepper
- 1/2 cup chopped celery
- 1/4 cup butter
- 1 1/2 cups cooked crabmeat
- 2 cups cooked rice
- 3 cups cooked eggplant, cut into cubes
- 1 can (4 ounces) mushrooms
- 1/2 teaspoon salt
- 1/2 teaspoon black pepper
- 1/2 teaspoon seasoned salt

1. Sauté onion, red bell pepper, green bell pepper, and celery in butter.
2. Add crabmeat and simmer until done.
3. Add cooked rice, cooked eggplant, and mushrooms. Season with salt, pepper, and seasoned salt.
4. Pour into casserole dish 13" x 9" x 2".
5. Garnish with parsley, if desired.

Yield: 5 cups
Makes 6 servings

Each serving contains:

Calories	211	Protein	10 g
Carbohydrate	22.7 g	Sodium	1070 mg
Total Fat	9.3 g	Cholesterol	61 mg
		Saturated Fat	4.9 g

Kirk Joseph Fruge

Rice & Seafood Casserole

- 1/2 cup chopped onion
- 2/3 cup chopped green bell pepper
- 2 small garlic cloves, chopped
- 1 cup chopped celery
- 1/4 cup chopped parsley
- 1 jar (2 ounces) chopped pimiento
- 1/4 cup butter
- 2 teaspoons salt
- 1/2 teaspoon red pepper
- 2 teaspoons black pepper
- 1 can (10 3/4 ounces) cream of mushroom soup
- 1 cup cooked crabmeat
- 1 cup cooked shrimp, shelled and deveined
- 3 cups cooked rice
- 1/2 cup breadcrumbs

1. Sauté onion, green bell pepper, garlic, celery, parsley, and pimiento in butter.
2. Add salt, red pepper, and black pepper.
3. Mix until blended.
4. Add soup and stir well.
5. Add crabmeat, shrimp, and rice, mixing well.
6. Pour into greased casserole dish and top with breadcrumbs.
7. Bake 20 minutes in oven at 400 degrees F.

Makes 10 servings

Each serving contains:

Calories	217	Protein	13.1 g
Carbohydrate	23 g	Sodium	1236 mg
Total Fat	7.9 g	Cholesterol	84 mg
		Saturated Fat	3.3 g

Shadd Taylor

Rice Chicken

1. Preheat oven to 350 degrees F.
2. Cook chicken in water until tender.
3. Let cool, debone, and cut meat in chunks.
4. Sauté onion and garlic in Lou Ana Vegetable Oil until wilted; let cool.
5. Mix chicken, onion, garlic, and rice.
6. Add mushrooms, water chestnuts, cream of celery soup and chicken stock to mixture.
7. Mix well.
8. Pour in greased 9" x 9" x 2" pan.
9. Sprinkle with breadcrumbs.
10. Cook for 30 minutes or until brown.
11. Serve as a main dish with a green salad.

Yield: 9 cups
Makes 10 servings

Each serving contains:

Calories	215	Protein	14.9 g
Carbohydrate	21.5 g	Sodium	726 mg
Total Fat	7.4 g	Cholesterol	36 mg
		Saturated Fat	1.9 g

Jo Vinson

1 chicken, approximately 3 pounds

3 cups chopped onion

2 medium garlic cloves, chopped

2 tablespoons Lou Ana Vegetable Oil

2 cups cooked rice

1 can (4 ounces) sliced mushrooms, drained

1 can (8 ounces) sliced water chestnuts, drained

1 can (10 3/4 ounces) cream of celery soup

1 can (14 ounces) chicken stock

1/2 cup seasoned breadcrumbs

TONY D. CHAMPAGNE

Party in Kentwood 'Til the Cows Come Home

It's a party 'til the cows come home in Kentwood, known throughout the South for its pure spring water, on the first weekend of every June.

The Kentwood Dairy Festival annually salutes the local dairy industry with a celebration that began as Dairy Day shortly after World War II.

In 1983 Dairy Day was expanded into a weekend-long festival featuring a Chef's Gala Cookoff and Food Fair, as well as the crowning of a beauty queen and an ice cream-eating contest. For the more serious dairy aficionados, there is a dairy calf show and a calf-calling contest.

But, food remains a big drawing card at this festival. Local amateur chefs flex their culinary muscles and vie for the gourmet crown, with well-known chefs and media personalities serving as judges. The public then is invited to choose the best for themselves. A food fair, featuring the contest entries as well as dishes prepared by local and visiting chefs, is open to the public for a nominal fee.

Kentwood is located in Tangipahoa Parish, northeast of Baton Rouge, near the Mississippi border.

Custard Ice Cream

- 1 quart whole milk, divided
- 2 cups sugar
- 8 eggs, well-beaten
- 48 ounces evaporated milk
- 2 teaspoons vanilla extract
- Whole milk to fill freezing container about 2/3 full (approximately 2 1/3 cups)

1. Bring 3 cups of whole milk and sugar to a boil.
2. Gradually pour into eggs while stirring.
3. Cook egg/milk mixture in top of double boiler over bottom of the boiler that contains simmering water. Cook until mixture coats metal spoon.
4. Cool. Add evaporated milk, one cup of whole milk, and vanilla extract.
5. Pour into 5-quart freezer bucket.
6. Add whole milk to fill freezer bucket 2/3 full.
7. Freeze.

Yield: 5 quarts
Makes 40 servings (1/2 cup each)

Each serving contains:
Calories 130
Carbohydrate ...... 15.7 g
Total Fat ....5.2 g
Protein .... 5.1 g
Sodium .... 72 mg
Cholesterol .... 59 mg
Saturated Fat .... 2.9 g

Judy Fowler
Ice Cream Category, 1986

Homemade Ice Cream

8 eggs

1 cup sugar

6 cups whole milk, divided

2 teaspoons vanilla extract

2 cans (14 ounces each) sweetened condensed milk

2 cups peaches, crushed

1. Beat eggs with mixer.
2. Add sugar. Mix well.
3. Add four cups of whole milk and mix well.
4. Place in top of double boiler and place over simmering water in bottom of double boiler.
5. Cook until mixture coats metal spoon. (It thickens only slightly.)
6. Add vanilla, remaining two cups of whole milk, and sweetened condensed milk. Pour into can of 4-quart ice cream freezer. (It should be 3/4 full.)
7. Freeze in hand-crank or electric ice cream freezer. After about fifteen minutes of freezing, add crushed peaches.

Yield: 4 quarts
Makes 32 servings (1/2 cup each)

Each serving contains:

Calories	160	Protein	5.1 g
Carbohydrate	23.7 g	Sodium	72 mg
Total Fat	5.2 g	Cholesterol	84 mg
		Saturated Fat	2.8 g

Flora Crawford
Ice Cream Category, 1986

Strawberry Ice Cream

- 2 cans (14-ounce size) condensed milk
- 3 cans (12-ounce size) evaporated milk
- 1 package (16-ounce) frozen strawberries, thawed and crushed
- 2 cans (12-ounce size) strawberry soda

1. Mix all ingredients together.
2. Freeze in 5-quart ice cream freezer.

Yield: 5 quarts
Makes 40 servings (1/2 cup each)

Each serving contains:

Calories	121	Protein	3.5 g
Carbohydrate	18.7 g	Sodium	58 mg
Total Fat	3.9 g	Cholesterol	15 mg
		Saturated Fat	2.4 g

Donna Miller
Ice Cream Category, 1986

Super Low-Fat Yogurt

- 1 cup boiling water
- 1/2 cup non-fat dry milk powder
- 1/2 cup fresh skim milk
- 3 tablespoons plain low-fat yogurt

1. Mix boiling water and dry milk in blender on low speed.
2. Add cold skim milk and blend again on low speed.
3. Blend in the yogurt.
4. Pour into glass or plastic containers and place in warm place (80 - 100 degrees F.) overnight. (A gas oven in which the pilot is burning is ideal. If you have a dehydrator, it works beautifully on about 100 degrees).
5. Refrigerate until served.

Yield: 2 cups
Makes 2 servings

Each serving contains:

Calories	89	Protein	8.5 g
Carbohydrate	12.6 g	Sodium	135 mg
Total Fat	0.4 g	Cholesterol	6 mg
		Saturated Fat	0.2 g

Maxie Slaton
Ice Cream Category, 1986

Toasted Almond Fudge

1 cup slivered almonds

3 cups sugar

2/3 cup evaporated milk

3/4 cup butter

1 1/2 cups marshmallow crème

12 ounces semi-sweet chocolate chips

1/2 teaspoon vanilla extract

1. Toast almonds at 450 degrees F. for about 5 minutes or until lightly toasted. Set aside.
2. Combine sugar, milk, and butter in large heavy saucepan. Heat until boiling.
3. Stir constantly over medium heat or until mixture reaches soft-ball stage. (About 5 minutes)
4. Remove from heat.
5. Add marshmallow crème and stir.
6. Add chocolate chips and vanilla extract and stir vigorously until well-blended.
7. Stir in almonds.
8. Pour into buttered 9" x 13" pan.
9. Cool and cut into 36 pieces.

Makes 36 pieces

Each piece contains:

Calories	189	Protein	1.6 g
Carbohydrate	26.9 g	Sodium	48 mg
Total Fat	9.5 g	Cholesterol	12 mg
		Saturated Fat	4.7 g

Donna Miller
First Place, Candy Category, 1987

Illey's Freezer Ice Cream

- 2 eggs, well-beaten
- 2 cans (14 ounces each) sweetened condensed milk
- 6 cups whole milk, divided
- 3 cans (5 ounces each) evaporated milk
- 2 teaspoons vanilla extract

1. Beat eggs with a mixer.
2. Beat in the two cans of sweetened condensed milk and two cups of whole milk. Pour into top of double boiler.
3. Place top of double boiler over simmering water in bottom of double boiler.
4. Cook until mixture coats metal spoon. (It thickens only slightly.)
5. Add four cups of whole milk, evaporated milk, and vanilla. Blend well.
6. Pour into the can of a 4-quart ice cream freezer. (It should be no more than 3/4 full.)
7. Freeze in hand-crank or electric ice cream freezer.

Variation: Add 2 small cans of crushed pineapple, 4 ripe bananas (mashed) or 1 1/2 cups of sliced ripe fresh strawberries.

Yield: 4 quarts
Makes 32 servings (1/2 cup each)

Each serving contains:

Calories	133	Protein	4.9 g
Carbohydrate	17.2 g	Sodium	74 mg
Total Fat	5.2 g	Cholesterol	37 mg
		Saturated Fat	3.2 g

Dr. Illey Dillon
Ice Cream Category, 1987

Orange Sherbert

1. Mix sweetened condensed milk and evaporated milk.
2. Add 2 orange drinks; mix well.
3. Add pineapple; mix well.
4. Pour into 5-quart freezer bucket.
5. Add orange drinks until freezer is 2/3 full.
6. Freeze as any ice cream.
7. Pack down after freezing for about 15 minutes before serving.

- 1 can (14 ounces) sweetened condensed milk
- 1 can (12 ounces) evaporated milk
- 6 cans (12 ounces each) Orange Crush drinks, divided
- 1 can (8 ounces) crushed pineapple

Yield: 5 quarts
Makes 40 servings (1/2 cup each)

Each serving contains:

Calories	73	Protein	1.4 g
Carbohydrate	13.9 g	Sodium	29 mg
Total Fat	1.6 g	Cholesterol	6 mg
		Saturated Fat	0.9 g

Ferrie Gene Blackmon
Ice Cream Category, 1986

Chocolate Ice Cream

1. Pour in a 4-quart freezer in this order: condensed milk, Cool Whip, chocolate milk.
2. Freeze according to instructions for electric or old-timey ice cream freezer.

- 1 can (14 ounces) condensed milk
- 1 carton (12 ounces) Cool Whip
- 2 quarts chocolate milk

Yield: 4 quarts
Makes 32 servings (1/2 cup each)

Each serving contains:

Calories	111	Protein	3.1 g
Carbohydrate	15.6 g	Sodium	56 mg
Total Fat	4.1 g	Cholesterol	8 mg
		Saturated Fat	3.3 g

Marie Hendry
Ice Cream Category, 1986

Old-Time Cocoa Fudge

- 1/3 cup cocoa
- 3 cups sugar
- 1/8 teaspoon salt
- 1 1/2 cups milk
- 6 tablespoons light corn syrup
- 1/4 cup butter
- 1 teaspoon vanilla extract
- 1 cup pecans

1. Butter 9" x 9" x 2" pan. Set aside.
2. Mix cocoa, sugar, and salt in a 3-quart saucepan.
3. Add milk and corn syrup, mix thoroughly. Bring mixture to a boil on a high heat setting.
4. Reduce to medium heat setting and continue to boil syrup until it reaches a temperature of 234 degrees F. or until a small amount of mixture forms a soft ball when dropped into cold water.
5. Remove from heat; add butter and vanilla extract.
6. Allow mixture to cool undisturbed about 15 minutes.
7. Beat with spoon until thick (hand mix).
8. Stir in pecans.
9. Quickly pour fudge into a lightly buttered 9" x 9" x 2" pan. Cool.
10. Cut into 16 pieces for serving.

Makes 16 pieces

Each piece contains:
Calories 256
Carbohydrate ...... 46.4 g
Total Fat .... 8.5 g
Protein .... 1.7 g
Sodium .... 64 mg
Cholesterol .... 11 mg
Saturated Fat .... 2.8 g

Bernice Fedele
Fourth Place, Candy Category, 1987

Hot Fudge Sauce

1. Mix sugar, salt, and cocoa. Add water. Blend well.
2. Stir in sweetened condensed milk.
3. Heat only until sugar dissolves, about 2 minutes. (This mixture burns easily; you may want to use a double boiler. If using a double boiler, have water boiling briskly while heating the mixture.)

4. Add vanilla extract.
5. Store in the refrigerator. Heat before serving.

Great on ice cream or cake!

Yield: About 2 cups
Serving size: 2 tablespoons

Each serving contains:

Calories	107	Protein	2.2 g
Carbohydrate	20.4 g	Sodium	48 mg
Total Fat	2.3 g	Cholesterol	8 mg
		Saturated Fat	1.5 g

Alma Allen
Ice Cream Category, 1987

1/2 cup sugar

1/8 teaspoon salt

1/4 cup cocoa

2 tablespoons water

1 can (14 ounces) sweetened condensed milk

1 teaspoon vanilla extract

Shrimp Mold

- 1 can (10 3/4 ounces) tomato soup
- 8 ounces cream cheese
- 2 envelopes unflavored gelatin (hydrated in 2 tablespoons of water)
- 1 cup mayonnaise
- 1 pound finely chopped cooked shrimp
- 1 cup diced celery
- 1 cup diced onion
- Dash of Tabasco sauce
- 2 tablespoons horseradish, drained
- 1 1/4 teaspoons salt

1. Heat soup.
2. Add cream cheese and stir until cheese is melted. (This mixture will be lumpy.)
3. Add hydrated gelatin.
4. Stir in mayonnaise and then remaining ingredients.
5. Pour into a 9-cup mold sprayed with vegetable cooking oil spray.
6. Refrigerate until set.
7. Unmold and serve with crackers as an appetizer.

Yield: 25 appetizer servings

Each serving contains:
Calories 139
Carbohydrate .... 3.1 g
Total Fat .... 11 g
Protein .... 7.5 g
Sodium .... 315 mg
Cholesterol .... 65 mg
Saturated Fat .... 3.9 g

Ruby Dillon
First Place, Appetizers, 1987

Potato Lover's Casserole

- 2 pounds frozen hash brown potatoes
- 1/2 cup butter, melted
- 1/2 pint sour cream
- 1/2 cup chopped onion
- 2 cups grated cheddar cheese
- 1 can (10 3/4 ounces) undiluted cream of chicken soup
- 1 teaspoon salt
- 3/4 teaspoon black pepper
- 2 cups crushed corn flakes
- 1/2 cup butter, melted

1. Preheat oven to 350 degrees F.
2. Place 2 pounds of frozen hash brown potatoes in a greased 9" x 13" pan.
3. Melt one-half cup of butter and pour over potatoes. Set aside.
4. In a 2-quart bowl, mix sour cream, onion, cheese, soup, salt, and black pepper.
5. Pour over potatoes and mix well.
6. Combine 2 cups of crushed corn flakes and the other 1/2 cup of melted butter.
7. Spread over potato mixture.
8. Bake one hour.

Yield: 9 cups
Makes 18 servings (1/2 cup each)

Each serving contains:

Calories	255	Protein	5.3 g
Carbohydrate	18.1 g	Sodium	549 mg
Total Fat	18.1 g	Cholesterol	48 mg
		Saturated Fat	11 g

Nancy Sansom
First Place, Vegetable Category, 1986

TONY O. CHAMPAGNE

Ruston

Peach Festival in Ruston: All-American Family Fun

Located in the picturesque rolling hills of north-central Louisiana is Ruston, home of the annual Louisiana Peach Festival.

The festival is held in June, when the commercial peach orchards of Lincoln Parish are bulging with the fruit of this multi-million dollar industry.

Since 1947 peaches have been an important crop in this part of Louisiana, and in 1951 the first Peach Festival was held to spread the word about the unexcelled taste of Lincoln Parish peaches.

The festival has grown from a two-day affair to a 10-day extravaganza featuring everything from a hot air balloon "glow," to a peach cookery contest to an art show to a fishing tournament just for kids. The festival has made the Southeast Tourism Society's list of the top 20 tourism events in the Southeast for several years running.

The festival agenda includes the Louisiana Peach Festival parade, beauty contests, a musical revue, dinner dance and a variety of athletic events, including archery, karate, softball and wheelchair racing.

Fresh peaches are sold throughout the festival in bushels, pecks and lugs. Peach ice cream is available in cones or gallons from the dairy at Louisiana Tech University located in Ruston.

Over 25 varieties of peaches are grown in the area, and many festival-goers leave with their share. Demonstrations, cooking contests and educational information ensures that they know how to eat, cook and preserve their peaches once at home.

Grand Champion Cobbler

1 cup all-purpose flour

1/2 teaspoon salt

1/3 cup shortening

1/4 cup milk

PASTRY

1. In a 2-quart bowl mix flour and salt for pastry.
2. Cut in shortening with a pastry blender until particles are the size of small peas.
3. Gradually add milk to form a dough. Stir only until mixture holds together.
4. Chill dough.
5. Roll chilled dough into a 10" x 10" square on floured board.
6. Preheat oven to 350 degrees F.

1 cup sugar

1/4 cup all-purpose flour

9 fresh peaches, peeled and sliced

1/4 cup butter

FILLING

1. In a 2-quart bowl, mix sugar and flour.
2. Add peaches. Stir until peaches are coated with the sugar-flour mixture.
3. Pour peach mixture into a 9" x 9" x 2" baking dish.
4. Dot with butter.
5. Top with pastry.
6. Cut several slits in pastry.
7. Bake in preheated oven 40 to 45 minutes or until light brown.

Makes 9 servings

Each serving contains:
Calories 281
Carbohydrate ...... 43.8 g
Total Fat .... 11.5 g
Protein .... 2.4 g
Sodium .... 156 mg
Cholesterol .... 14 mg
Saturated Fat .... 4.2 g

Mrs. L. C. Colvin
Grand Prize Cobbler, 1959 and 1987

Spicy Peach Cobbler

- 8 peaches, peeled and sliced
- 2 tablespoons lemon juice
- 3/4 cup sugar
- 1/4 cup all-purpose flour
- 1 teaspoon cinnamon
- 1 teaspoon ground ginger
- Pastry for double crust

1. Preheat oven to 425 degrees F.
2. Combine sliced peaches and lemon juice; toss.
3. Combine sugar, flour, cinnamon, and ginger; add to peaches, mixing lightly.
4. Set the mixture aside.
5. Divide the pastry into two equal portions. Roll one portion to 1/8-inch thickness on a lightly floured surface. Fit into a 9-inch square pastry dish.
6. Spoon peach mixture evenly into prepared pastry shell.
7. Roll out remaining pastry to 1/8-inch thickness; cut into 1/2-inch strips. Lay half the strips across the filling, spacing them about 3/4-inch apart.
8. Repeat with remaining strips, arranging them to form lattice work.
9. Bake for 10 minutes; reduce heat to 350 degrees, and bake an additional 40 minutes.

Makes 9 servings (3" x 3")

Each serving contains:

Calories	323	Protein	3.3 g
Carbohydrate	45.7 g	Sodium	241 mg
Total Fat	14.9 g	Cholesterol	0 mg
		Saturated Fat	2.9 g

Kelly Pesnell
Boys and Girls Division, 1987

Peach Cobbler

- 2/3 cup sugar
- 2 tablespoons all-purpose flour
- 2 cups peeled and sliced fresh peaches
- 1 uncooked pie crust

1. Preheat oven to 350 degrees F.
2. Mix sugar and flour.
3. Add peaches, mix and pour into 8" x 8" x 2" baking dish.
4. Cut pie crust into strips.
5. Place strips of crust on top of peach mixture in criss-cross pattern.
6. Bake for 40 minutes or until brown.

Makes 8 servings (2" x 4")
Serves 8

Each serving contains:
Calories 271
Carbohydrate ...... 48.1 g
Total Fat .... 8.6 g
Protein .... 2.5 g
Sodium .... 139 mg
Cholesterol .... 0 mg
Saturated Fat .... 1.7 g

Elvie Westbrook
Ladies Division, 1987

Peach Pie

- 3 cups peeled and sliced fresh peaches
- 1 tablespoon lemon juice
- 3/4 cup sugar
- 3 tablespoons all-purpose flour
- 3 tablespoons butter
- Pastry for 2 pie crusts

1. Preheat oven to 350 degrees F.
2. Mix together peaches and lemon juice.
3. Mix sugar and flour.
4. Add sugar mixture to peaches.
5. Place peach mixture in uncooked pie crust in 8" pie plate.
6. Dot top of peaches with butter.
7. Cut remaining pastry in strips and construct lattice top over peaches.
8. Bake for approximately one hour.

Yield: One 8-inch pie
Makes 6 servings

Each serving contains:

Calories	493	Protein	4.5 g
Carbohydrate	64.9 g	Sodium	376 mg
Total Fat	25.3 g	Cholesterol	16 mg
		Saturated Fat	7.4 g

Bessie Gillenwater
Grand Prize, Peach Pie Category, 1981

Peach of a Pie

- 1 - 9" pie shell, baked
- 1 package (8 ounces) cream cheese
- 3 tablespoons sugar
- 1/4 teaspoon salt
- 1 tablespoon milk
- 1/2 teaspoon vanilla extract
- 3/4 cup sugar
- 2 tablespoons cornstarch
- 1 1/2 cups crushed strawberries
- 2 tablespoons lemon juice
- 1 can (1lb.-13 oz.) peach halves
- 1 1/2 cups halved strawberries

1. In a medium bowl, thoroughly blend cream cheese with 3 tablespoons of sugar, salt, milk, and vanilla extract.
2. Using back of teaspoon, carefully spread cheese mixture over bottom of cooled, baked pie shell.
3. In a 2-quart saucepan, blend 3/4 cup of sugar and cornstarch.
4. Add strawberries and lemon juice.
5. Cook over medium heat, stirring constantly, until mixture is clear and thickened; cool, stirring occasionally.
6. Carefully arrange peach halves around outside edge of pie.
7. In center, place strawberry halves.
8. Spoon strawberry mixture over peaches and strawberries.
9. Refrigerate until serving time.

Yield: One 9-inch pie
Makes 8 servings

Each serving contains:
Calories 347
Carbohydrate ...... 42.5 g
Total Fat .... 18.7 g
Protein .... 4.2 g
Sodium .... 312 mg
Cholesterol .... 32 mg
Saturated Fat .... 8 g

Mariam Hammons Stone
Ladies Division, 1987

Peachy Fruit Pizza

CRUST

1. Preheat oven to 350 degrees F.
2. Press cookie dough into 13" x 9" pan.
3. Bake until done.
4. Cool.

1 roll sugar cookie dough

FILLING

1. Beat cream cheese and confectioners sugar.
2. Spread over cooled crust.
3. Arrange peaches on top.

8 ounces cream cheese

1/2 cup confectioners sugar

1 1/2 cans (16-ounce size) peach slices, drained (Fresh peaches can be used.)

GLAZE

1. In a 1-quart saucepan, combine orange juice, lemon juice, water, sugar, and cornstarch.
2. Cook over medium heat until clear.
3. Cool and pour over peaches.

1/2 cup orange juice

1/4 cup lemon juice

3/8 cup water

1/2 cup sugar

2 tablespoons cornstarch

Yield: 20 pieces (2" x 2 1/2" each)
Makes 20 servings

Each serving contains:			
Calories	186	Protein	1.9 g
Carbohydrate	25.2 g	Sodium	144 mg
Total Fat	9.1 g	Cholesterol	20 mg
		Saturated Fat	3.8 g

Jenny Shea
Boys and Girls Division, 1987

Peach Glaze Cheesecake

2 tablespoons butter

3/4 cup vanilla wafer crumbs

CRUST

❶ Preheat oven to 350 degrees F.

❷ Mix butter and crumbs together.

❸ Place in 9" pie plate and press in bottom and up sides.

❹ Bake for five minutes.

12 ounces cream cheese, softened

1/2 cup sugar

1 teaspoon lemon juice

2 eggs

1/2 cup sour cream

1/2 cup finely chopped peaches

FILLING

❶ Mix together cream cheese, sugar, and lemon juice in a mixing bowl.

❷ Add eggs. Beat well.

❸ Stir in sour cream and peaches.

❹ Pour mixture into crust.

❺ Bake for 25 minutes or until set.

❻ Cool in refrigerator.

❼ Cover with a fresh peach glaze or preserves, if desired.

Yield: One 9-inch cheesecake
Makes 8 servings

Each serving contains:
Calories 252
Carbohydrate ...... 15.6 g
Total Fat .... 19.3 g
Protein .... 5.2 g
Sodium .... 151 mg
Cholesterol .... 122 mg
Saturated Fat ..... 11.7 g

Russ Hilton
Boys and Girls Division, 1987

Peaches & Cream Dessert

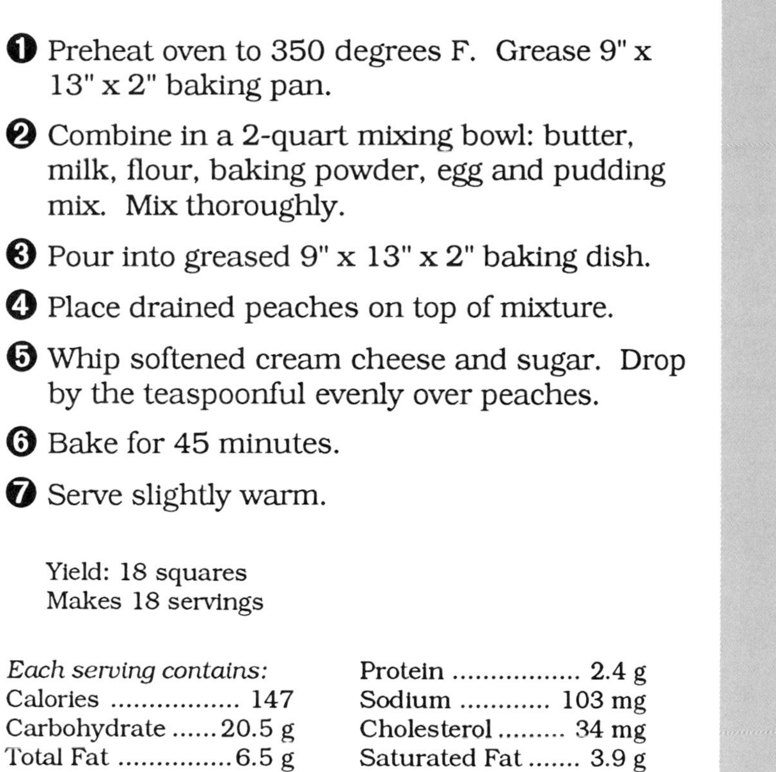

1. Preheat oven to 350 degrees F. Grease 9" x 13" x 2" baking pan.
2. Combine in a 2-quart mixing bowl: butter, milk, flour, baking powder, egg and pudding mix. Mix thoroughly.
3. Pour into greased 9" x 13" x 2" baking dish.
4. Place drained peaches on top of mixture.
5. Whip softened cream cheese and sugar. Drop by the teaspoonful evenly over peaches.
6. Bake for 45 minutes.
7. Serve slightly warm.

Yield: 18 squares
Makes 18 servings

Each serving contains:

Calories	147	Protein	2.4 g
Carbohydrate	20.5 g	Sodium	103 mg
Total Fat	6.5 g	Cholesterol	34 mg
		Saturated Fat	3.9 g

Mrs. Debra Tisdale
Grand Champion Winner, 1987

2 tablespoons butter

3/4 cup milk

3/4 cup all-purpose flour

1 tablespoon baking powder

1 egg, beaten

1 package (3 ounces) vanilla pudding

4 cups canned peach slices

8 ounces cream cheese

3/4 cup sugar

Peach Pound Cake

- 1 cup butter
- 3 cups sugar
- 6 eggs
- 1 teaspoon vanilla extract
- 1/2 teaspoon almond extract
- 3 cups all-purpose flour
- 1/4 teaspoon baking soda
- 1/2 teaspoon salt
- 1/2 cup sour cream
- 2 cups chopped peaches
- Confectioners sugar (to dust top after baking)

1. Preheat oven to 325 degrees F. Grease and flour a 10-inch tube pan.
2. In a large mixer bowl, cream butter and sugar until fluffy.
3. Add eggs, one at a time, and beat after each addition.
4. Stir in vanilla extract and almond extract.
5. In a small bowl combine dry ingredients; add to creamed mixture.
6. Fold in sour cream and peaches.
7. Pour batter into prepared pan. Bake 75 to 85 minutes or until toothpick comes out clean.
8. Dust with confectioners sugar, if desired.

Yield: One 10-inch cake
Makes 16 servings

Each serving contains:
Calories 417
Carbohydrate ...... 64.5 g
Total Fat .... 15.5 g
Protein .... 6.1 g
Sodium .... 238 mg
Cholesterol .... 137 mg
Saturated Fat .... 8.8 g

Larry Jarrell
Men's Division, 1987

Peach Salad

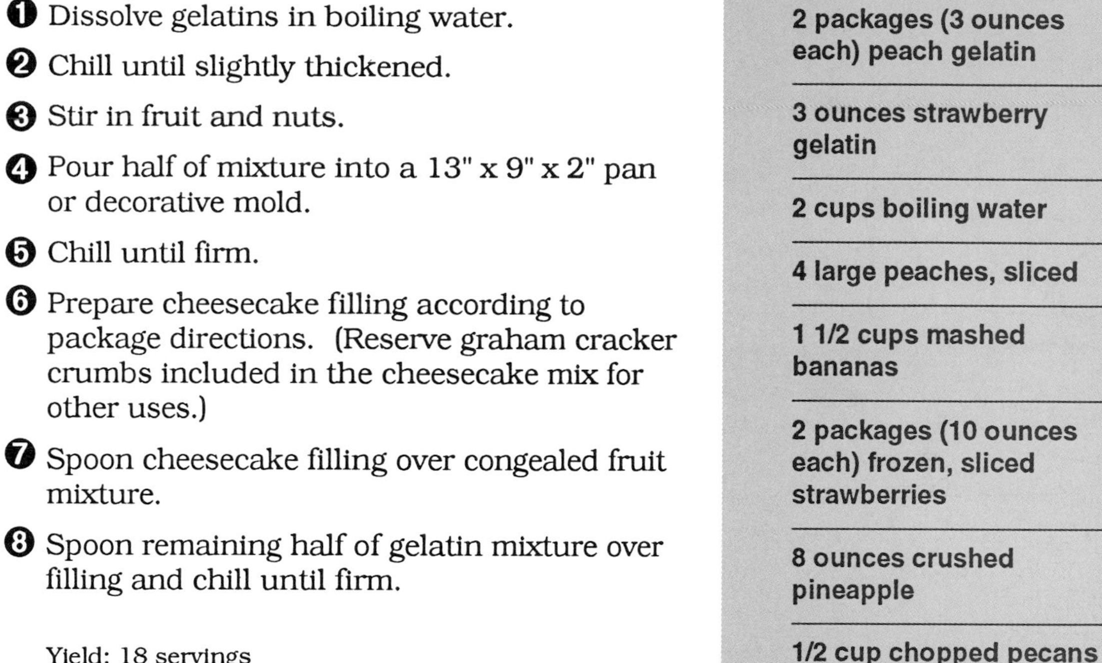

1. Dissolve gelatins in boiling water.
2. Chill until slightly thickened.
3. Stir in fruit and nuts.
4. Pour half of mixture into a 13" x 9" x 2" pan or decorative mold.
5. Chill until firm.
6. Prepare cheesecake filling according to package directions. (Reserve graham cracker crumbs included in the cheesecake mix for other uses.)
7. Spoon cheesecake filling over congealed fruit mixture.
8. Spoon remaining half of gelatin mixture over filling and chill until firm.

2 packages (3 ounces each) peach gelatin

3 ounces strawberry gelatin

2 cups boiling water

4 large peaches, sliced

1 1/2 cups mashed bananas

2 packages (10 ounces each) frozen, sliced strawberries

8 ounces crushed pineapple

1/2 cup chopped pecans

1 package (10.5 ounces) cheesecake mix

Yield: 18 servings

Each serving contains:

Calories	209	Protein	3.6 g
Carbohydrate	42.8 g	Sodium	158 mg
Total Fat	3.9 g	Cholesterol	0 mg
		Saturated Fat	0.1 g

Kay Bond
Boys and Girls Division, 1987

Scottish Peach Bars

CRUST

- 2 cups all-purpose flour
- 1/2 cup confectioners sugar
- 1/2 teaspoon salt
- 1 cup butter, softened
- 1 cup chopped pecans

1. Preheat oven to 350 degrees F.
2. In a 2-quart bowl mix flour, confectioners sugar and salt together.
3. Cut in butter.
4. Stir in pecans.
5. Pat into jelly roll pan.
6. Bake until lightly browned (approximately 15 minutes).
7. Cool.

TOPPING

- 11 ounces cream cheese (8-ounce package and 3-ounce package)
- 1/2 cup confectioners sugar
- 1 1/2 cups frozen whipped topping, thawed
- 1 can (24 ounces) sliced peaches (Fresh peaches can be used if available.)
- 1 can (3 1/2 ounces) coconut, toasted

1. After crust has completely cooked, prepare topping.
2. Combine cream cheese and confectioners sugar.
3. Fold in whipped topping.
4. Spread evenly over the cooked crust.
5. Cut each peach slice into about 4 pieces and evenly distribute over the top of the cream cheese mixture.
6. Sprinkle toasted coconut evenly over peaches.
7. Chill thoroughly.
8. Cut into bars and serve.

Yield: 40 bars

Each bar contains:

Calories	148	Protein	1.8 g
Carbohydrate	11.3 g	Sodium	101 mg
Total Fat	11.1 g	Cholesterol	21 mg
		Saturated Fat	6.5 g

Sandee Sledge
Ladies Division, 1987

Peachy Apricot Mold

1 package (3 ounces) apricot gelatin

1 cup boiling water

1/2 cup cold water

1 package (8 ounces) cream cheese, softened

2 cups sliced peaches

❶ Dissolve apricot gelatin in 1 cup of boiling water. Add 1/2 cup of cold water. Set aside to cool.

❷ Beat softened cream cheese until smooth. Add about 1/4 cup of prepared apricot gelatin and beat until smooth. Add remainder of gelatin. Mix well.

❸ Place cream cheese-gelatin mixture in the refrigerator until mixture begins to thicken.

❹ Fold in 2 cups of sliced peaches. If canned peaches are used, drain well before folding into gelatin mixture and cut peach slices into 4 pieces each.

❺ Pour into a 4-cup mold (or 9" x 9" x 2" container).

❻ Chill until firm.

❼ Unmold on salad plate (or cut in squares to serve) and garnish as desired.

Makes 8 servings

Each serving contains:

Calories	168	Protein	3.7 g
Carbohydrate	17.1 g	Sodium	121 mg
Total Fat	10.2 g	Cholesterol	32 mg
		Saturated Fat	6.3 g

Joan Maulden
Ladies Division, 1987

Keystone Krunch

1 quart thin cream

2 teaspoons vanilla extract

1/2 cup sugar

1/8 teaspoon salt

ICE CREAM

1. Mix cream, vanilla extract, sugar, and salt.
2. Chill for 30 minutes and freeze in ice cream freezer.

1 can (5 ounces) roasted, slivered almonds

6 ounces vanilla wafers, crumbled fine

CRUMB MIXTURE

1. Combine vanilla wafer crumbs and almonds.
2. Set aside.

4 cups well-mashed, fresh peaches

1 teaspoon Fruit Fresh

1/4 cup sugar

PEACH MIXTURE

1. Combine peaches, Fruit Fresh, and sugar.
2. Set aside.

ASSEMBLING KEYSTONE KRUNCH

1. Put one-third of the crumb mixture in the bottom of a 9" x 13" x 2" pan.
2. Spread half of the ice cream evenly on top of crumbs.
3. Spread half of the peach mixture evenly over ice cream.

4. Repeat crumb layer, ice cream layer, and peach layer. Top with remaining third of crumb mixture.

5. Freeze until firm.

6. Cut into pieces approximately 2" x 3"

Makes 16 servings

Each serving contains:

Calories	318	Protein	4.4 g
Carbohydrate	26.7 g	Sodium	76 mg
Total Fat	22.8 g	Cholesterol	64 mg
		Saturated Fat	10.4 g

Allen Tutten
Grand Champion, 1971

TONY O. CHAMPAGNE

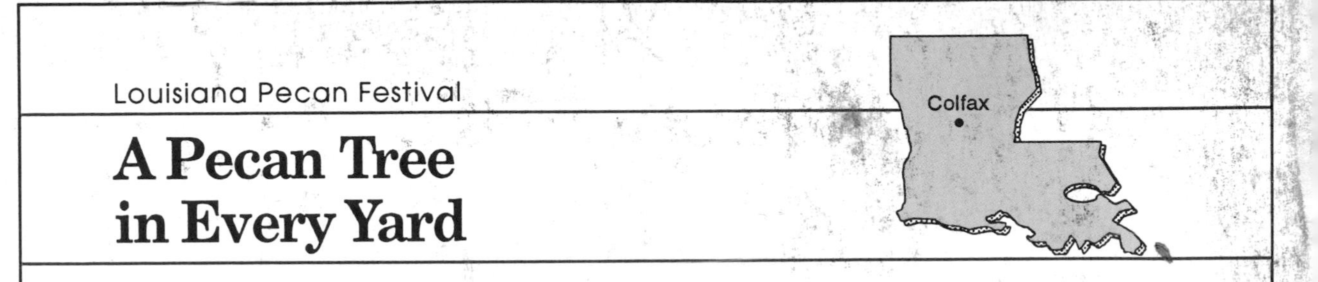

A Pecan Tree in Every Yard

Travelers driving on Highway 8 along the Red River during the first weekend in November are apt to see horse-drawn wagons and fashions from the 1880s as they approach the town of Colfax.

These are all elements of the annual Pecan Festival, which began in 1969 as part of the town's centennial celebration. Today, townspeople and visitors alike celebrate the harvesting of the pecans, a profitable crop to this farming and lumber community of just over 2,000.

The Caddo Indians who lived along the banks of the Red River taught the white settlers to plant and harvest pecans. In the years since, pecan trees have multiplied to the point that virtually every yard in Colfax has at least one pecan tree.

The festival begins on Friday morning with the Blessing of the Crops. The rest of the morning is devoted to arts and crafts, cooking contests, costume contests and the presentation of the Queen and her court, who were selected in contests in October. The bands kick off around 1 p.m. and play until nightfall, when the trail riders arrive.

The Grand Parade starts Saturday at 9 a.m., followed by afternoon dance performances by the "Pecanettes" and concerts by the local high school bands and choirs. The latter half of the day is devoted to Cajun and Top 40 music, and the festival concludes with a fireworks display.

Marsha's Pecan Pie

1 cup sugar

3 tablespoons cornstarch

3 tablespoons butter

1 cup dark corn syrup

3 eggs, beaten

1 tablespoon vanilla extract

1 teaspoon vinegar

1 cup chopped pecans

1 unbaked pie shell (9-inch)

1. Preheat oven to 350 degrees F.
2. Mix sugar and cornstarch.
3. Add butter and cream mixture together.
4. Add syrup, beaten eggs, vanilla extract, and vinegar. Mix well.
5. Stir in chopped pecans.
6. Pour mixture into pie shell and place on large cookie sheet.
7. Place on middle rack in oven and bake for 30 minutes or until set.

Yield: One 9-inch pie
Makes 8 servings

Each serving contains:
Calories 508
Carbohydrate ...... 70.2 g
Total Fat .... 23.9 g
Protein .... 4.7 g
Sodium .... 283 mg
Cholesterol .... 114 mg
Saturated Fat .... 5.7 g

Marsha Krause

Pecan Crunchies

1 bar (8 ounces) milk chocolate

1 1/4 cups prepared whipped topping

1 cup chopped toasted pecans

1/2 cup finely crushed vanilla wafers

1. Break chocolate bar into small squares in a 1-quart microwave-safe casserole dish.
2. Micro-cook, uncovered, on 100% power (high) for 1 1/2 to 2 minutes, stirring once.
3. Remove from microwave. Stir until smooth.
4. Fold in whipped topping and pecans. (Mixture will thicken.)
5. Cover and chill at least 1 hour.
6. Form into balls 1 inch in diameter.
7. Roll in vanilla wafer crumbs.
8. Chill thoroughly.

Yield: 26 balls

Each ball contains:

Calories	92	Protein	0.8 g
Carbohydrate	6.6 g	Sodium	8 mg
Total Fat	7.4 g	Cholesterol	2 mg
		Saturated Fat	3.1 g

Kaycee Carter

Bourbon-Pecan Pound Cake

- 2 cups butter
- 3 cups sugar
- 8 large eggs, separated
- 2 teaspoons vanilla extract
- 2 teaspoons almond extract
- 1/4 cup bourbon
- 3 cups all-purpose flour
- 2 cups chopped pecans

1. Preheat the oven to 300 degrees F.
2. Line the bottom of a 10-inch tube pan with wax paper. Grease sides well.
3. Cream the butter and sugar together.
4. Add the egg yolks, one at a time, beating well after each addition.
5. Mix extracts and bourbon. Alternately add the flour and the liquids.
6. In another bowl, beat the egg whites until stiff, then fold into the batter.
7. Sprinkle the bottom of the cake pan with half the pecans, then pour in the batter.
8. Sprinkle the top of the batter with the remaining pecans.
9. Bake for 1 1/2 hours.
10. Allow the cake to cool, then remove from pan. You may let it set for a day or two before serving.

Note: This cake does not have a chemical leavening agent (baking powder or baking soda), therefore ingredients must be creamed well during preparation.

Yield: One 10-inch pound cake
Makes 20 slices

Each slice contains:

Calories	466	Protein	5.6 g
Carbohydrate	47.6 g	Sodium	212 mg
Total Fat	28.2 g	Cholesterol	159 mg
		Saturated Fat	12.8 g

Mrs. Q. A. Hargis, Jr.

Sand Tarts

1 cup butter

1/2 teaspoon vanilla extract

6 tablespoons confectioners sugar

2 cups all-purpose flour

1/4 teaspoon salt

1 cup finely chopped pecans

1. Preheat oven to 300 degrees F.
2. In a 2-quart bowl, cream butter, vanilla extract, and sugar.
3. In a 1-quart bowl, sift together flour and salt.
4. Mix together creamed ingredients and flour mixture.
5. Add chopped pecans. Mix well. Form dough into a ball.
6. Break off pieces of dough and shape into crescents. Place crescents on ungreased baking sheet.
7. Bake until light brown, approximately 20 minutes.
8. Roll warm cookies in additional confectioners sugar, if desired.

Yield: 25 tarts

Each tart contains:

Calories	141	Protein	1.6 g
Carbohydrate	10.9 g	Sodium	99 mg
Total Fat	10.4 g	Cholesterol	20 mg
		Saturated Fat	4.8 g

Connie Youngblood

TONY O. CHAMPAGNE

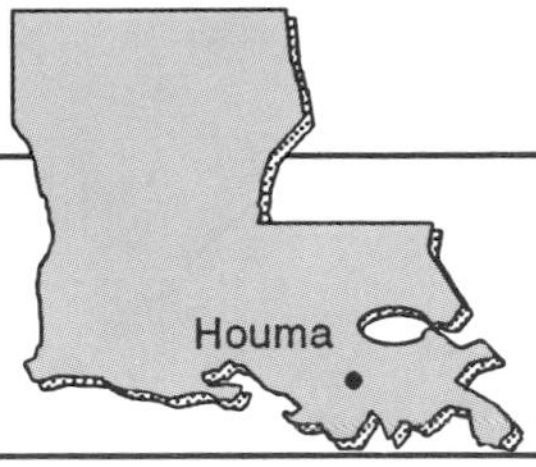

The World's Largest Praline Was Made Here

Houma

The praline, a sugary candy made with pecans, is one of Louisiana's most popular sweets.

The Louisiana Praline Festival, held annually in Houma on the first weekend in May, pays tribute to the praline and its part in Louisiana's rich history.

The first pralines were probably made in France during the reign of Louis XIII. Records show that Count Pessis-Prasline served a confection of almonds rolled in cooked sugar to his guests, who begged for the recipe. Because the candy didn't have a name yet, it was dubbed "praslines" after its inventor.

Early French settlers in Louisiana brought to their new home a love of pralines, but substituted native pecans when almonds proved difficult to obtain.

The Praline Festival began in 1964; it was originally called the May Day Fair. The festival is held on the St. Gregory School grounds, and proceeds benefit the church and school.

Each year brings something new to the festivities. Part of the fun at the 1987 festival was viewing and tasting the world's largest praline: 98.2 pounds of creamy, delicious candy.

Annual praline competitions inspire contestants to create new versions of this old favorite. Past versions have included the addition of dates, coconut and even sweet potatoes.

Festival-goers won't go hungry at this festival. Booths sell such culinary delights as crawfish fettuccine, fried catfish, seafood gumbo and shrimp etouffee.

Festival-goers can work off a few calories dancing to live Cajun and Zydeco music or shopping for homemade crafts. A carnival and fireworks display add to the fun.

Basic Pecan Pralines

- 2 2/3 cups sugar
- 1 cup evaporated milk
- 1/2 cup butter
- 2 tablespoons white corn syrup
- 2 cups pecan halves
- 1 teaspoon vanilla extract

1. In a 2-quart heavy saucepan, mix sugar, evaporated milk, butter, and corn syrup.
2. Cook until a teaspoonful of the mixture forms a soft ball (235 degrees F.) when dropped in water.
3. Remove from heat and add pecans and vanilla extract.
4. Beat until very thick and heavy.
5. Drop by the teaspoonful onto waxed paper placed on cloth. (This makes pralines easier to pick up.)

Yield: 30 pralines

Each praline contains:

Calories	140	Protein	1 g
Carbohydrate	18.4 g	Sodium	37 mg
Total Fat	7.5 g	Cholesterol	9 mg
		Saturated Fat	2.4 g

Mae St. Marie

Date-Pecan Pralines

- 4 1/2 cups brown sugar
- 2 cups milk
- 2 tablespoons white corn syrup
- 3 tablespoons butter
- 1 cup chopped dates
- 1 cup chopped pecans
- 1 teaspoon vanilla extract

1. In a 2-quart heavy saucepan, mix brown sugar, milk, corn syrup, and butter.
2. Cook slowly until a teaspoonful of the mixture forms a soft ball (235 degrees F.) when dropped into a cup of cool water.
3. Remove from heat.
4. Add the dates, pecans, and vanilla extract.
5. Let mixture cool for a minute or two, then beat with spoon until thickened and creamy.
6. Immediately drop by the tablespoon onto a damp cloth.
7. Remove when cold.

Yield: 36 pralines

Each praline contains:

Calories	158	Protein	0.8 g
Carbohydrate	32.4 g	Sodium	27 mg
Total Fat	3.5 g	Cholesterol	5 mg
		Saturated Fat	1.1 g

Rosadelle D. Melancon
Second Place, 1985

Coconut-Pecan Pralines

- 4 cups sugar
- 1/2 cup butter
- 1 cup evaporated milk
- 3 tablespoons corn syrup
- 3 cups fresh, grated coconut
- 3 cups finely chopped pecans
- 1/2 teaspoon vanilla extract

1. In a heavy 3-quart saucepan, mix sugar, butter, milk, and corn syrup.
2. Cook over medium heat until mixture thickens.
3. Add coconut and pecans.
4. Cook to a temperature of 248 degrees F. (A firm ball will form when a teaspoonful of the syrup is dropped in cold water.)
5. Remove from heat and add vanilla extract.
6. Beat until thickened.
7. Drop by the teaspoonful onto waxed paper.

Yield: 48 pralines

Each praline contains:

Calories	172	Protein	1.3 g
Carbohydrate	20.6 g	Sodium	29 mg
Total Fat	10.3 g	Cholesterol	7 mg
		Saturated Fat	4.9 g

Mae St. Marie
First Place, 1985

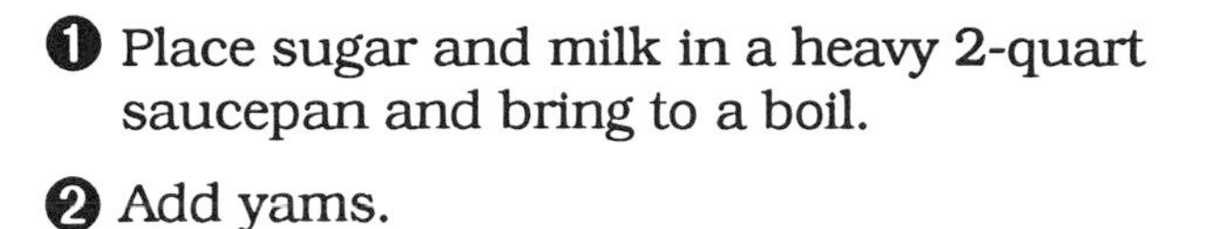

Sweet Potato Pralines

- 2 cups sugar
- 1/2 cup evaporated milk
- 1/2 cup cooked, mashed yams
- 1 cup pecans
- 1/4 cup butter
- 1/2 teaspoon vanilla extract

1. Place sugar and milk in a heavy 2-quart saucepan and bring to a boil.
2. Add yams.
3. Cook until mixture reaches 235 degrees F. (soft-ball stage).
4. Remove from heat and add pecans, butter, and vanilla extract.
5. Let cool.
6. Beat and pour into a buttered 8" x 8" dish.
7. Allow to completely harden. Cut and serve.

Yield: 20 pieces

Each piece contains:

Calories	148	Protein	1 g
Carbohydrate	22.9 g	Sodium	31 mg
Total Fat	6.5 g	Cholesterol	8 mg
		Saturated Fat	2 g

Chris Viguerie

TONY O. CHAMPAGNE

Competitive Spirit Prevails at Rapides Parish Fair

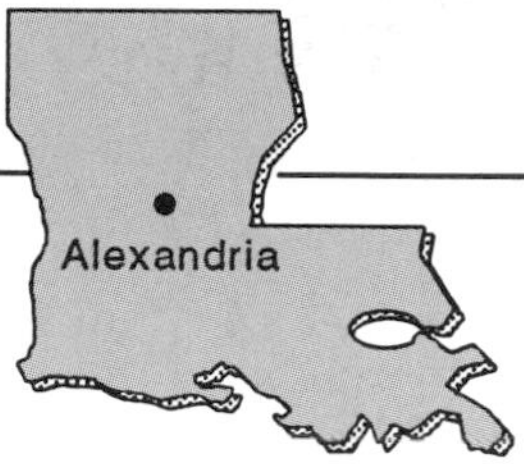

Alexandria

The Rapides Parish Fair, held the second week of October, is an old-fashioned blend of baking, sewing and livestock competitions combined with a sizzling carnival midway.

The fair, which began in 1960 in Alexandria, is one of the most outstanding parish fairs in Louisiana. The winners of the various contests in Alexandria go on to compete at the state fair level in Shreveport and often bring home ribbons.

One of the most consistent winners at the parish level is 83-year-old Mrs. D.A. Robicheaux, who has accumulated more than 3,000 awards since the Rapides Parish Fair began. In 1989 she received 48 first places, 40 second and eight third.

In its early years the fair was held under tents in an open muddy field west of Alexandria. It was always too dusty or too muddy, and within a few years the Rapides Parish Coliseum was built on the site.

Today the crafts, home improvement displays and agricultural exhibits are showcased in the coliseum's air-conditioned exhibit hall, while the animals are housed in nearby buildings.

The 4-H division is one of the most popular, particularly since it involves fair animals ranging from pint-sized rabbits to mountainous-looking steers.

Records show that some 50,000 people visit the exhibits each year, and it is estimated that at least five times this many go to the carnival, which brings to this central Louisiana city exciting rides and entertainment.

German Chocolate Cake

2 cups sugar
1/2 cup shortening
3 egg yolks
4 ounces German sweet chocolate
1/2 cup boiling water
2 1/2 cups all-purpose flour
1/4 teaspoon salt
1 teaspoon baking soda
1 1/4 cups buttermilk
1 teaspoon vanilla extract
3 egg whites

CAKE

1. Preheat oven to 350 degrees F.
2. Cream sugar and shortening until fluffy.
3. Add egg yolks, one at a time.
4. Melt chocolate in boiling water; add to creamed mixture.
5. Combine flour, salt, and soda; add flour mixture alternately with buttermilk to creamed mixture.
6. Add vanilla extract.
7. Fold in stiffly beaten egg whites.
8. Pour into three greased and floured 9-inch cake pans.
9. Bake for about 30 minutes or until done.
10. Cool cake in pans for 10 minutes; then remove from pans.
11. Finish cooling on rack.
12. Spread Filling between layers and on top of cake.

1 1/2 cups sugar
1 1/2 cups evaporated milk
3/4 cup butter
4 egg yolks
2 cups flaked coconut
1 1/3 cups pecans, chopped
2 teaspoons vanilla extract

FILLING

1. Combine sugar, evaporated milk, butter, and egg yolks and cook over low heat until thickened. Stir constantly.
2. Remove from heat; add coconut, pecans, and vanilla. Mix well, then cool until thickened.

Yield: One 9-inch, three-layer cake
Makes 20 servings

Each serving contains:
Calories 485
Carbohydrate ...... 55.1 g
Total Fat .... 28.2 g
Protein .... 6.2 g
Sodium .... 182 mg
Cholesterol .... 120 mg
Saturated Fat ..... 13.1 g

Mrs. Eschol Bruyninchx
First Place, German Chocolate Cakes, 1988

Coconut Pound Cake

- 1 cup butter
- 1/2 cup Lou Ana Vegetable Oil
- 3 cups sugar
- 5 eggs
- 3 cups sifted all-purpose flour
- 1/2 teaspoon baking powder
- 1/2 teaspoon salt
- 1 cup milk
- 1 teaspoon vanilla extract
- 1 teaspoon coconut flavoring
- 3 1/2 ounces flake coconut

❶ Preheat oven to 325 degrees F.

❷ Cream butter and oil. Add sugar gradually and cream well after each addition.

❸ Add eggs, one at a time. Beat well after each egg is added.

❹ Sift flour, baking powder and salt together. Add alternately with milk.

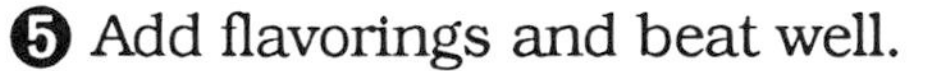

❺ Add flavorings and beat well.

❻ Stir in coconut. Pour into a long loaf pan or a large tube pan (12 cups) that has been greased and floured.

❼ Bake for about 1 1/2 hours.

Yield: 36 slices

Each slice contains:

Calories	205	Protein	2.3 g
Carbohydrate	25 g	Sodium	101 mg
Total Fat	11 g	Cholesterol	53 mg
		Saturated Fat	5.9 g

Mrs. Eschol Bruyninchx
First Place, Pound Cakes, 1988

Devil's Food Cake

- 1 cup butter
- 2 cups sugar
- 3 eggs
- 2 1/2 cups cake flour
- 1/4 cup half and half cream
- 1/2 cup buttermilk
- 1 teaspoon baking soda
- 1 teaspoon baking powder
- 1/4 cup cocoa
- 1 cup boiling water
- 1 teaspoon vanilla extract

- 1 box (16 ounces) confectioners sugar, sifted
- 8 teaspoons cocoa
- 1/2 cup butter
- 1/4 cup black coffee
- 1 tablespoon vanilla extract

CAKE

1. Preheat oven to 350 degrees F.
2. Grease 3 round cake pans (8-inch) and line bottoms with waxed paper.
3. Cream butter and sugar and blend in beaten eggs.
4. Add 1/2 cup cake flour.
5. Add cream, mixed with buttermilk.
6. Combine remaining cake flour, baking soda, and baking powder; sift together.
7. Dissolve cocoa in boiling water. Cool. Add to batter alternately with flour mixture.
8. Add vanilla.
9. Bake at 350 degrees F. for 20 to 25 minutes.
10. Cool completely.
11. Spread Frosting between layers, on sides and on top of cake.

FROSTING

1. Sift confectioners sugar and cocoa together. Set aside.
2. Cream butter.
3. Add confectioners sugar and cocoa to butter. Mix well.
4. Add coffee and vanilla extract. Mix well.

Yield: One 3-layer (8-inch) cake
Makes 16 servings

Each serving contains:

Calories	444	Protein	3.2 g
Carbohydrate	66.9 g	Sodium	264 mg
Total Fat	19.4 g	Cholesterol	100 mg
		Saturated Fat	11.6 g

Mrs. Eschol Bruyninchx
First Place, Chocolate Layer Cakes, 1988

Mile-High Biscuits

 Preheat oven to 450 degrees F.

2. Combine first five ingredients, mixing well; cut in shortening with pastry blender until mixture resembles coarse meal.

3. Combine egg and milk, add to flour mixture. Stir until dry ingredients are moistened.

4. Turn dough on floured surface and knead 8 to 10 times.

5. Roll to 3/4-inch thickness; cut into biscuits with 2 1/2-inch diameter cutter.

6. Bake on ungreased sheet at 450 degrees for 15 minutes or until golden brown.

Yield: 20 biscuits

Each biscuit contains:

Calories	162	Protein	3 g
Carbohydrate	17.6 g	Sodium	153 mg
Total Fat	8.8 g	Cholesterol	16 mg
		Saturated Fat	1.6 g

Helen G. Foreman
First Place, Biscuits, 1988

3 cups all-purpose flour

2 tablespoons sugar

1 tablespoon baking powder

3/4 teaspoon cream of tartar

1 teaspoon salt

3/4 cup shortening

1 egg

1 1/4 cups milk

Creamy Pralines

- 1 1/4 cups sugar
- 3/4 cup brown sugar
- 1/2 cup evaporated milk
- 1/2 cup pecans
- 2 tablespoons butter
- 1 teaspoon vanilla extract

1. Mix sugars and milk in heavy saucepan.
2. Cook over low heat, stirring until sugar is thoroughly dissolved.
3. Continue cooking until mixture forms a soft ball when dropped in cold water, about 5 minutes (cook to 234 degrees F.).
4. Remove from heat and stir in pecans.
5. Add butter and vanilla extract.
6. Beat until candy just begins to thicken.
7. Drop quickly from a tablespoon onto a waxed paper or oiled surface.
8. If candy becomes too stiff to drop into smooth patties, stir in a small amount of hot water a few drops at a time until mixture is the consistency desired.

Yield: 25 pralines

Each praline contains:

Calories	89	Protein	0.5 g
Carbohydrate	16.2 g	Sodium	17 mg
Total Fat	2.8 g	Cholesterol	4 mg
		Saturated Fat	0.9 g

Naomi Samples
First Place, Candy Division

Divinity

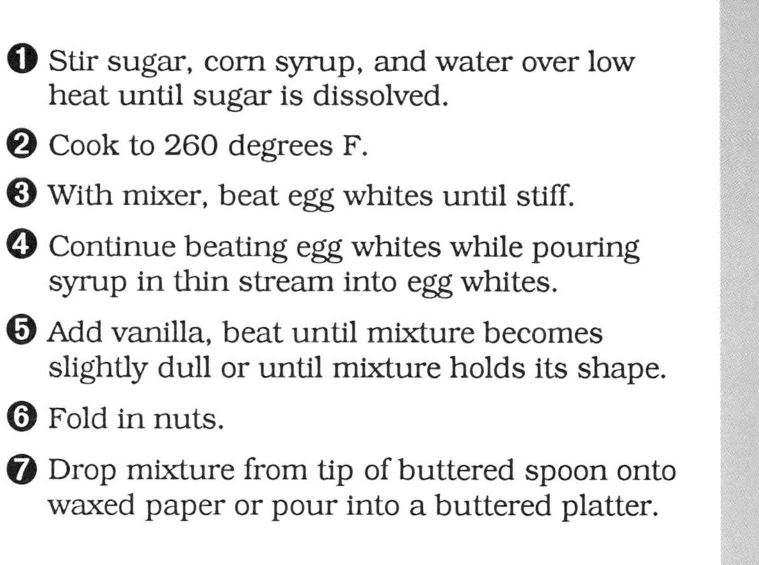

1. Stir sugar, corn syrup, and water over low heat until sugar is dissolved.
2. Cook to 260 degrees F.
3. With mixer, beat egg whites until stiff.
4. Continue beating egg whites while pouring syrup in thin stream into egg whites.
5. Add vanilla, beat until mixture becomes slightly dull or until mixture holds its shape.
6. Fold in nuts.
7. Drop mixture from tip of buttered spoon onto waxed paper or pour into a buttered platter.

Yield: 50 pieces

Each piece contains:

Calories	83	Protein	0.5 g
Carbohydrate	14.6 g	Sodium	9 mg
Total Fat	2.9 g	Cholesterol	0 mg
		Saturated Fat	0.2 g

Mrs. Jerome Vanderlick
First Place, Divinity Candy, 1988

- 2 2/3 cups sugar
- 2/3 cup light corn syrup
- 1/2 cup water
- 2 egg whites
- 1 teaspoon vanilla extract
- 2 cups chopped pecans

Choco-Mint Fudge

- 1 1/2 cups sugar
- 2/3 cup evaporated milk
- 1/4 cup butter
- 7 ounces marshmallow crème
- 1 bag (12 ounces) semi-sweet chocolate chips
- 3/4 cup pecans
- 1 teaspoon peppermint flavoring

1. In medium saucepan, combine sugar, evaporated milk, and butter.
2. Bring to full boil, stirring constantly, over moderate heat.
3. Boil 5 minutes, stirring constantly, over moderate heat.
4. Remove from heat.
5. Stir in marshmallow crème and chocolate chips. Stir until chips are completely melted and mixture is smooth.
6. Stir in pecans and peppermint flavoring.
7. Pour into foil-lined 8-inch square pan.
8. Chill in refrigerator until firm.
9. Cut into 1 1/4-inch squares.

Yield: 36 squares (1 1/4 inches)
Makes 36 servings

Each serving contains:

Calories	131	Protein	1 g
Carbohydrate	19.1 g	Sodium	22 mg
Total Fat	6.5 g	Cholesterol	5 mg
		Saturated Fat	3 g

Ms. Edith Petrus

Everything But The Kitchen Sink Cookies

1. Preheat oven to 375 degrees F.
2. Cream sugar, brown sugar, butter, and shortening together.
3. Mix in eggs and vanilla extract.
4. Add flour and oat bran. Mix well.
5. Stir in remaining ingredients.
6. Drop by the rounded teaspoon onto an ungreased cookie sheet.
7. Bake for 10 minutes or until golden brown.

Yield: 10 dozen cookies

Each cookie contains:

Calories	65	Protein	0.8 g
Carbohydrate	7.8 g	Sodium	43 mg
Total Fat	3.7 g	Cholesterol	7 mg
		Saturated Fat	1.5 g

Susan Hurley

- 1 cup sugar
- 1 cup brown sugar
- 1/2 cup butter
- 1/2 cup butter-flavored Crisco
- 2 eggs
- 2 teaspoons vanilla extract
- 2 1/4 cups self-rising flour
- 1/4 cup oat bran
- 1 package (12 ounces) mini chocolate chips
- 1/2 cup chopped walnuts
- 1/2 cup chopped pecans
- 1/2 cup coconut
- 1 cup oatmeal
- 1/4 cup wheatgerm

Louisiana Honey-Pecan Pie

9-inch unbaked pastry shell

3 eggs

1/2 cup sugar

1/2 cup corn syrup

1/2 cup honey

1/4 cup butter

1 teaspoon vanilla extract

2 tablespoons white cornmeal

1 teaspoon white vinegar

2 cups chopped pecans

1. Preheat oven to 350 degrees F. Combine eggs, sugar, corn syrup, honey, melted butter, and vanilla extract.
2. Mix until blended.
3. Add cornmeal, vinegar, and pecans.
4. Mix thoroughly.
5. Pour into unbaked pie shell.
6. Cover with aluminum foil and bake until firm (about 1 hour).
7. Uncover and continue baking until slightly brown.

Yield: One 9-inch pie
Makes 8 servings

Each serving contains:
Calories 548
Carbohydrate ...... 60.7 g
Total Fat .... 33.7 g
Protein .... 5.9 g
Sodium .... 223 mg
Cholesterol .... 118 mg
Saturated Fat .... 7.2 g

Colleen L. Dunn
First Place, 1988

Carrot-Honey Bread

1. Preheat oven to 325 degrees F. Grease and flour bundt pan.* Set aside.
2. Beat eggs, honey, brown sugar and Lou Ana Vegetable Oil. Set aside.
3. Combine both kinds of flour, baking powder, salt, ginger, cinnamon, and oats.
4. Stir egg mixture into dry ingredients until just moistened.
5. Fold in carrots and pecans.
6. Spoon batter into greased and floured bundt pan.
7. Bake about 50 minutes. (Check after 45 minutes.)
8. Cool on wire rack 10 minutes; turn out and cool thoroughly.

* Pan must be well-greased and -floured.

Yield: 24 slices

Each slice contains:

Calories	228	Protein	3.2 g
Carbohydrate	25.4 g	Sodium	132 mg
Total Fat	13.3 g	Cholesterol	34 mg
		Saturated Fat	2.8 g

Helen G. Foreman
First Place, Quick Breads, 1988

- 3 eggs
- 2/3 cup honey
- 1/2 cup brown sugar
- 2/3 cup Lou Ana Vegetable Oil
- 1 cup all-purpose flour
- 1 cup whole wheat flour
- 1 tablespoon baking powder
- 1 teaspoon salt
- 1 teaspoon ginger
- 1 tablespoon cinnamon
- 1 cup rolled oats
- 2 cups grated carrots
- 1 cup chopped pecans

TONY O.CHAMPAGNE

Oldest of State's Agricultural Festivals Still Going Strong

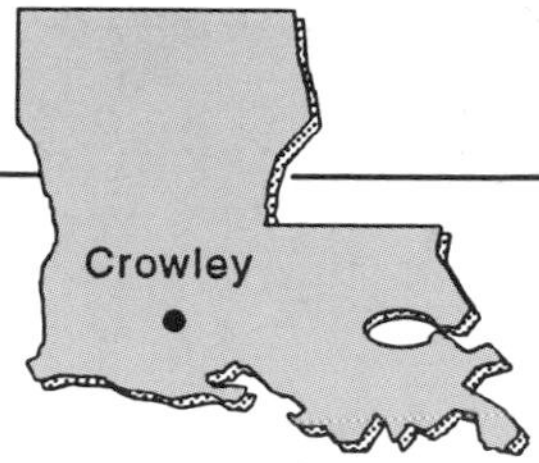

Crowley

The International Rice Festival is Louisiana's oldest agricultural festival, and annually thousands swell the streets of Crowley for this October celebration.

The first festival was held in 1937 to boost the state's rice industry. That same year also marked Crowley's 50th anniversary, "the Golden Jubilee." A double public wedding was held at that first festival with the festival's rice princesses serving as bridesmaids. The festival was destined to become an annual event, except during the years of World War II when it was postponed.

Over the years various celebrities have shared in the festival fun, including the late John F. Kennedy and his wife, Jacqueline, in 1959, as well as Ed McMahon and the Clydesdale horses.

Parkerson Avenue in downtown Crowley is where much of this festival's action takes place. Friday's schedule includes the popular children's parade in which area school children ride on homemade floats.

Food stalls are put up along the length and breadth of the parade route and offer food and drinks. A carnival spirit and appetizing smells permeate the cool October air.

Some of the festival's original traditions remain, including the livestock show, rice-grading competition and a window-decorating contest. Some newer activities that draw a crowd are the accordion, harmonica and fiddle contests and the rice-threshing demonstration at the Rice Museum.

Broccoli, Meat & Rice Casserole

1 package (10 ounces) frozen chopped broccoli

1/2 cup water

1/2 pound ground chuck

1 cup chopped onion

1 can (10 3/4 ounces) condensed cream of mushroom soup

6 slices American cheese

1 1/2 cups cooked rice

1/4 cup unseasoned breadcrumbs

1. Preheat oven to 350 degrees F.
2. Cook broccoli in water. Drain and set aside.
3. Brown meat with onion in skillet.
4. In small saucepan, combine cream of mushroom soup and cheese. Cook over medium heat until cheese melts.
5. In casserole dish, combine broccoli, meat mixture and cooked rice.
6. Pour sauce over dish and mix lightly.
7. Sprinkle with breadcrumbs.
8. Bake for 30 minutes.

Makes 8 servings (3/4 cup each)

Each serving contains:

Calories 224
Carbohydrate ...... 17.7 g
Total Fat .... 10.9 g
Protein .... 14.1 g
Sodium .... 653 mg
Cholesterol .... 40 mg
Saturated Fat .... 5.2 g

Michelle Comeaux
First Place, Children's Division, 1988

Shrimp, Broccoli & Rice Casserole

1/4 cup butter

1 cup chopped onion

1 cup chopped celery

1/2 cup chopped green bell pepper

1 cup raw shrimp, peeled and deveined

8 ounces pasteurized processed cheese spread

1 can (10 3/4 ounces) condensed cream of mushroom soup

1 package (10 ounces) frozen chopped broccoli

3 cups cooked rice

1/4 teaspoon garlic powder

1/2 teaspoon Tabasco sauce

1. Preheat oven to 350 degrees F.
2. In melted butter, sauté onion, celery, and green bell pepper until translucent.
3. Add shrimp. Cook until shrimp are pink.
4. Add cheese, soup, broccoli, rice, garlic powder, and Tabasco sauce. Mix well.
5. Pour into buttered 2 1/2-quart casserole dish.
6. Bake for 30 minutes or until bubbly.

Makes 7 servings (1 cup each)

Each serving contains:

Calories	373	Protein	20.7 g
Carbohydrate	31.2 g	Sodium	1281 mg
Total Fat	17.6 g	Cholesterol	120 mg
		Saturated Fat	9.2 g

Meredith Barras
First Place, Children's Division, 1988

Cajun Turnovers

- 1/2 cup chopped onion
- 1/4 cup chopped green bell pepper
- 1/4 cup chopped celery
- 2 tablespoons butter
- 1/2 cup chopped canned mushrooms
- 1 package long-grain wild rice mix (4.3-oz. size)
- 2 cups water
- 1 tablespoon Worcestershire sauce
- 2 teaspoons hot sauce
- 1/2 teaspoon garlic powder
- 1/2 teaspoon red pepper
- 2 cans crescent rolls
- 1 egg, beaten

1. Sauté onion, green bell pepper, and celery in butter until tender.
2. Add mushrooms.
3. Add rice and water. Stir.
4. Add Worcestershire sauce, hot sauce, garlic powder, and red pepper. Mix well.
5. Bring to a boil. Cover tightly. Simmer 10 minutes.
6. While rice is simmering, preheat oven to 375 degrees F.
7. Separate crescent rolls into rectangles. Seal the seams in each rectangle by pressing the dough together.
8. Place rice mixture* in the center of each rectangle.
9. Fold dough over and press with a fork to seal the edges.
10. Brush tops of turnovers with beaten egg. Place on lightly greased cookie sheet.
11. Bake 12 to 13 minutes.

*Turnovers are easier to shape if rice mixture is chilled.

Yield: 8 turnovers
Makes 8 servings

Each serving contains:
Calories 294
Carbohydrate ...... 35.9 g
Total Fat .... 14.5 g
Protein .... 5.3 g
Sodium .... 585 mg
Cholesterol .... 28 mg
Saturated Fat .... 2 g

Alicia Ruddock
First Place, Adult Division, 1988

Chicken, Vegetable & Rice Casserole

1. Preheat oven to 375 degrees F.
2. Cut cooked chicken into one-inch cubes. Set aside.
3. Sauté onion and celery in butter.
4. Mix sautéed vegetables, chicken, soup, mushrooms, pimiento, mayonnaise, cheese, and rice together.
5. Fold in green beans.
6. Pour all ingredients in a greased 13" x 9" x 2" casserole dish.
7. If desired, sprinkle more Parmesan cheese on top.
8. Bake until hot and bubbly (30 to 40 minutes).

Yield: 9 cups
Makes 12 servings (3/4 cup each)

Each serving contains:

Calories	385	Protein	15.2 g
Carbohydrate	17.3 g	Sodium	784 mg
Total Fat	28.4 g	Cholesterol	83 mg
		Saturated Fat	11 g

Ethel Miller
First Place, Adult Division, 1988

1 cooked fryer, bones and skin discarded

1 cup chopped onion

2 stalks celery, cut into 1/4-inch pieces

1/2 cup butter

1 can (10 1/2 ounces) cream of celery soup

4 ounces drained mushrooms

1 jar (2 ounces) pimientos

1 cup mayonnaise

1 cup grated Parmesan cheese

3 cups cooked rice

2 cans (16 ounces each) French-style green beans, drained

Fantastic Flounder

STUFFING

1/4 cup butter

1 cup chopped onion

1/4 cup chopped green bell pepper

1/2 cup chopped celery

1 garlic clove, minced

1 can (6 ounces) cooked crabmeat

1 pound chopped raw crawfish tails

2 cups cooked long-grain rice

1/2 cup chopped green onion tops

1/2 cup chopped parsley

1/2 teaspoon salt

1/2 teaspoon black pepper

1 beaten egg

FISH

1 1/2 pounds flounder fillets

1. Preheat oven to 350 degrees F.
2. Melt butter. Sauté onion, green bell pepper, celery, and garlic in melted butter.
3. Add crabmeat and crawfish. Mix well and heat until crawfish is cooked. Remove from heat.
4. Fold in rice, onion tops, parsley, salt and pepper.
5. Fold in beaten egg.
6. Place half of fillets on bottom of a 2 1/2-quart casserole dish.
7. Spoon stuffing on top of fillets.
8. Place remaining fillets on top of stuffing.

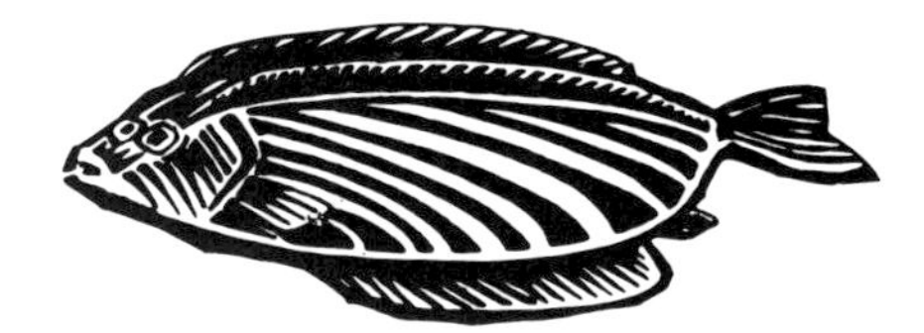

9. Mix all Sauce ingredients together.
10. Pour Sauce over stuffed flounder.
11. Bake about 35 minutes until flounder is done.

Note: Whole flounder may be used.

Makes 9 servings

Each serving contains:

Calories	332	Protein	26.8 g
Carbohydrate	15.5 g	Sodium	849 mg
Total Fat	17.8 g	Cholesterol	166 mg
		Saturated Fat	9.9 g

Josette Habetz
First Place (Chef de Ritz), Adults, 1988

SAUCE

1/2 cup butter

1/2 cup lemon juice

2 tablespoons Worcestershire sauce

1/4 cup chopped green onion tops

1/4 cup chopped parsley

Stuffed Catfish

- 1 tablespoon butter
- 1/4 cup onion
- 1/4 cup green bell pepper
- 1/4 cup chopped celery
- 5 ounces tomatoes with chilies
- 1/2 pound cooked shrimp, coarsely ground
- 1/2 cup cooked crabmeat
- 1 teaspoon Creole seasoning
- 1 cup cooked rice
- 2 fillets of catfish (1/2 pound)
- 1/4 teaspoon black pepper
- 1/4 cup green onion tops

❶ Preheat oven to 325 degrees F.

❷ Melt butter; sauté onion, green bell pepper, and celery.

❸ Add tomatoes.

❹ Stir in ground shrimp and crabmeat. Add Creole seasoning.

❺ Add cooked rice. Mix well.

❻ Sprinkle catfish fillets with black pepper.

❼ Place one catfish fillet in the bottom of a glass loaf pan (8 1/2" x 4 1/2" x 2 1/2") that has been sprayed with vegetable oil cooking spray.

❽ Place stuffing on top of fillet.

❾ Lay second catfish fillet on top of stuffing.

❿ Bake for 30 minutes or until done.

⓫ Garnish with green onion tops.

Makes 4 servings

Each serving contains:

Calories	285	Protein	32.5 g
Carbohydrate	15.5 g	Sodium	981 mg
Total Fat	10.4 g	Cholesterol	183 mg
		Saturated Fat	2 g

Lois Ann Mouton
First Place, Teen Division, 1988

Easy Crawfish-Rice Salad

- 3 cups cooked rice
- 1 pound cooked crawfish tails
- 4 hard-boiled eggs, chopped
- 3/4 cup mayonnaise
- 1 tablespoon mustard
- 2 tablespoons minced onion
- 2 tablespoons minced celery
- 2 tablespoons chopped pimientos
- 2 tablespoons chopped sweet pickle relish
- 1 teaspoon salt
- 1/4 teaspoon black pepper
- 1/8 teaspoon red pepper

1. Combine all ingredients in a large bowl. Mix well.
2. Refrigerate.
3. Serve on lettuce leaves.

Yield: 8 1/2 cups
Makes 8 servings

Each serving contains:

Calories	329	Protein	14.6 g
Carbohydrate	21.8 g	Sodium	820 mg
Total Fat	20.1 g	Cholesterol	206 mg
		Saturated Fat	5.3 g

Brandy Thevis
First Place, Intermediate Category, 1988

Rice-Stuffed Bell Peppers

- 5 green bell pepper hulls
- 1/4 pound ground chuck
- 1/4 pound ground pork
- 1/2 cup chopped onion
- 1/2 cup chopped green bell pepper
- 1 clove garlic, chopped
- 1/2 can (10 3/4-oz. size) mushroom soup
- 5 ounces of Rotel tomatoes with chilies
- 1 ounce pimiento
- 3/4 cup cooked long-grain white rice
- 1 cup cooked yellow rice

1. Preheat oven to 350 degrees F.
2. Partially cook hulls in boiling water (about 5 minutes).
3. Brown ground chuck and ground pork.
4. Add onion, pepper, and garlic. Cook until wilted.
5. Add mushroom soup and Rotel tomatoes. Cook 2 minutes.
6. Stir in pimiento, cooked long-grain white rice, and cooked yellow rice.
7. Stuff peppers.
8. Bake for 10 minutes.

Makes 5 servings

Each serving contains:

Calories	241	Protein	12.5 g
Carbohydrate	29.1 g	Sodium	389 mg
Total Fat	8.3 g	Cholesterol	30 mg
		Saturated Fat	2.7 g

Kimberly Fruge
First Place, Intermediate Category, 1988

Rice & Apricot Delight

- 3 tablespoons melted butter
- 1 cup coconut macaroon cookie crumbs
- 2 tablespoons sugar
- 1 cup sour cream
- 1 package unflavored gelatin
- 1 1/2 cups cooked rice
- 7 ounces marshmallow crème
- 1 cup pineapple sherbet
- 2 cups Cool Whip
- 1 teaspoon vanilla extract
- 1 can (15 ounces) apricot halves, drained
- 1/2 cup apricot preserves
- 1 tablespoon water

1. Combine melted butter, cookie crumbs, and sugar. Mix well.
2. Press mixture onto bottom of a spring form pan. Set aside.
3. Combine sour cream, gelatin, and rice in saucepan. Let stand for 3 minutes.
4. Bring to a boil; cook, stirring constantly until thickened and gelatin is dissolved. Remove from heat.
5. Stir in marshmallow crème; beat until smooth.
6. Add sherbet; mix well.
7. Fold in Cool Whip and vanilla extract.
8. Pour mixture over crust.
9. Chill until firm.
10. Arrange apricots in decorative pattern around top.
11. Beat apricot preserves and water until smooth and spoon over apricots as a glaze.

Makes 12 servings

Each serving contains:

Calories	292	Protein	2.7 g
Carbohydrate	49 g	Sodium	163 mg
Total Fat	10.1 g	Cholesterol	17 mg
		Saturated Fat	7.2 g

Mrs. Amson "Delta" Corner
First Place, Adult Division, 1988

Strawberry-Rice Pie

- 8 ounces cream cheese
- 1/2 cup sugar
- 1 package unflavored gelatin
- 1/4 cup strawberry juice
- 1 1/2 cups frozen strawberries, thawed
- 1 cup cooked rice
- 1/2 cup whipping cream, whipped
- 1 9-inch baked pie shell

1. Beat cream cheese and sugar until fluffy. Use electric mixer.
2. Dissolve gelatin in heated strawberry juice; cool to room temperature.
3. Combine with cheese mixture. (Make sure all lumps of cream cheese have disappeared.)
4. Stir in strawberries.
5. Stir in cooked rice. Chill mixture over ice water bath until thick, but not set.
6. Fold in whipped cream.
7. Pour into baked pie shell.
8. Chill and serve.

Yield: one 9-inch pie
Makes 8 servings

Each serving contains:
Calories 362
Carbohydrate ...... 34.3 g
Total Fat .... 23.3 g
Protein .... 5.4 g
Sodium .... 325 mg
Cholesterol .... 53 mg
Saturated Fat ..... 11.3 g

Annie Leger
First Place, Children's Division, 1988

Ultimate Strawberry-Rice Dessert

CRUST

- 6 egg whites
- 2 cups sugar
- 1 teaspoon baking powder
- 1 teaspoon vanilla extract
- 1 cup pecans
- 2 cups butter-flavored cracker crumbs

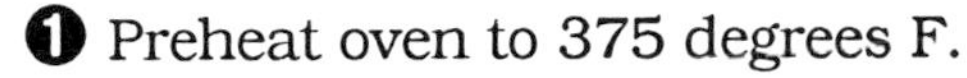

1. Preheat oven to 375 degrees F.
2. Beat egg whites to soft peaks; add sugar, baking powder, vanilla. Beat well. Fold in pecans and cracker crumbs.
3. Spread evenly in greased 13" x 9" x 2" baking dish.
4. Bake for 20 to 25 minutes. Let cool thoroughly.

FILLING

- 1/2 cup raw rice
- 1 1/2 cups water
- 1 tablespoon almond flavoring
- 1 tablespoon sugar
- 2 packages Dream Whip
- 1 cup milk
- 8 ounces cream cheese
- 1 cup crushed strawberries
- 1/2 cup chopped pecans

1. Cook raw rice in mixture of water, almond flavoring, and sugar. When cooked, refrigerate until chilled thoroughly.
2. Prepare Dream Whip with milk. Set aside.
3. Beat cream cheese. Add strawberries and beat again.
4. Combine cream cheese mixture and cooked rice. Fold in the Dream Whip.
5. Spread on cooled crust; sprinkle with pecans.
6. Refrigerate.
7. Garnish with fresh strawberries, if desired.

Makes 15 servings (approximately 3" x 2 1/2" each)

Each serving contains:

Calories	393	Protein	6.4 g
Carbohydrate	54.2 g	Sodium	166 mg
Total Fat	17.4 g	Cholesterol	17 mg
		Saturated Fat	4.3 g

Carla Pousson
First Place, Teen Division, 1988

TONY O. CHAMPAGNE

The Very Versatile Soybean: Something to Celebrate

Jonesville

The soybean, which first came to the United States from Japan as the "Japan pea," is the star of the annual Louisiana Soybean Festival in Jonesville.

The first Soybean Festival was staged back in 1956 to promote the soybean industry in Catahoula, Concordia and other adjoining parishes in Louisiana, where soybeans have gained prominence as an agricultural commodity. The festival was first part of the Catahoula Parish Fair, but it became an independent event in 1961.

The festival is held the second week in September, and begins with beauty contests for all ages. Food is a major attraction, and festival-goers can sample soybeans concocted into a variety of delectable dishes. But there's more on the menu, and booths with all kinds of goodies are on the festival grounds.

Tennis matches and golf rounds are part of the activities, and there are street dances, art exhibits, a craft show and a fireworks display on the Black River. The festival ends on Sunday with Gospel music and sand drag races.

What many festival-goers don't realize is that until 1911 the soybean was used primarily as a forage crop in America. At that time commercial processing of soybean seeds to obtain oil began, and improved methods of refining have developed a product that is excellent for use in shortening and margarine.

The versatile bean is showing up in more and more food products, and homemakers are becoming more aware that it is a high-protein, low-in-saturated-fat food source, say festival organizers.

The soybean also has industrial applications and is used in the production of high-grade enamels, sealants and caulking compounds, linoleum and oil cloth, pharmaceuticals and cosmetics.

Soya-Stuffed Mushrooms

- 1 pound fresh mushrooms
- 1 tablespoon butter
- 2 tablespoons chopped onion
- 2 tablespoons chopped celery
- 1/2 cup mashed cooked soybeans
- 2 tablespoons bread-crumbs
- 1/2 teaspoon Tabasco sauce
- 1 teaspoon Worcestershire sauce
- 1/2 teaspoon seasoned salt
- 1/4 teaspoon black pepper
- 2 ounces cheddar cheese, shredded

1. Preheat oven to 350 degrees F.
2. Clean mushrooms.
3. Remove and chop stems. Reserve caps.
4. In skillet, melt butter.
5. Add chopped stems, onion, and celery. Sauté until vegetables are tender.
6. Stir in remaining ingredients except cheese.
7. Fill mushroom caps with bean mixture and place on a greased baking sheet.
8. Bake for 15 minutes. Remove mushrooms from baking sheet and place in a microwave-safe serving dish.
9. Top each mushroom with shredded cheese. Place in microwave on lowest setting until cheese melts.
10. Serve warm.

Yield: Approximately 36 stuffed mushrooms (depending on size of mushrooms)

Each mushroom has:

Calories	17	Protein	1 g
Carbohydrate	1.2 g	Sodium	32 mg
Total Fat	1 g	Cholesterol	2 mg
		Saturated Fat	0.5 g

Laurie Stutson
First Place, Appetizer Category, 1984

Farmer's Salad

❶ Combine all of the ingredients.

❷ Mix well.

❸ Place in covered container.

❹ Refrigerate for 24 hours before serving.

Yield: 7 cups
Makes 9 servings

Each serving contains:			
Calories	273	Protein	6 g
Carbohydrate	15 g	Sodium	224 mg
Total Fat	22.2 g	Cholesterol	33 mg
		Saturated Fat	5.5 g

Ruby Nell Smith
First Place, Salads, 1984

2 cups canned whole-kernel corn, drained

2 cups cooked soybeans, drained

2 cups sliced celery

1 red onion, chopped

1 small jar sliced pimiento

1 cup mayonnaise

2 teaspoons sugar

1 teaspoon Italian seasoning

1/4 teaspoon garlic powder

Seasoned salt (a few grains)

1/8 teaspoon pepper

Cool Rise Rapid Mix White Bread

- 1 cup soya flour
- 5 1/2 cups all-purpose flour
- 2 packages active dry yeast
- 2 tablespoons sugar
- 1 tablespoon salt
- 1/4 cup soft butter
- 2 1/4 cups very hot tap water
- Lou Ana Vegetable Oil

1. Measure soya flour and all-purpose flour and blend together uniformly in a 3-quart bowl.
2. Combine 2 cups of the flour mixture, the dry yeast, sugar, and salt in large bowl. Stir well to blend. Add soft butter.
3. Add hot tap water to ingredients in bowl all at once. Beat with electric mixer at medium speed for 2 minutes. Scrape sides of bowl occasionally.
4. Stir in remaining flour gradually with wooden spoon. Use just enough flour to make a soft dough that leaves sides of bowl.
5. Turn out onto floured board. Round up into a ball.
6. Divide dough into 2 equal parts. Knead 5 to 10 minutes or until dough is smooth and elastic.
7. Cover with a plastic wrap and then a towel. Let rest for 15 to 20 minutes on board. Punch down.
8. Shape each portion into a loaf. Place in a greased 8" x 4" bread pan. Brush surface with Lou Ana Vegetable Oil.
9. Let dough rise until double in size. Puncture any surface bubbles with an oiled toothpick just before baking.

10. Bake for 35 minutes or until done in an oven preheated to 400 degrees F. Bake on a lower oven rack for best results.
11. Remove from pan immediately. Brush top crust with butter, if desired. Cool on rack.

Note: If using self-rising flour, omit salt.

Yield: 2 loaves (15 slices per loaf)

One slice contains:

Calories	122	Protein	3.8 g
Carbohydrate	21.1 g	Sodium	250 mg
Total Fat	2.4 g	Cholesterol	4 mg
		Saturated Fat	1 g

Lilly Montpelier
First Place, Breads, 1985

'Porcupines'

- 1/2 pound tofu and 1 1/2 pounds hamburger, or 2 pounds ground chuck
- 1/2 cup uncooked instant rice
- 1/2 cup chopped onion
- 1/2 cup chopped celery
- 1/2 cup chopped green bell pepper
- 1 egg
- 1 tablespoon Worcestershire sauce
- 2 teaspoons prepared mustard
- 1 1/2 teaspoons salt
- 1 can (10 3/4 ounces) cream of mushroom soup
- 1/2 cup water
- 1/4 cup catsup
- 1/2 cup cheddar cheese, grated

1. Preheat oven to 350 degrees F.
2. Combine meat(s), instant rice, onion, celery, and green bell pepper.
3. Add egg, Worcestershire sauce, mustard, and salt. Mix well.
4. Form into balls (about 25).
5. Place into a lightly greased shallow 2 1/2-quart casserole dish. Set aside.
6. Combine soup, water and catsup. Bring to a boil and pour over the meatballs.
7. Cover casserole dish and bake for one hour.
8. Remove from oven and sprinkle with cheese.
9. Cover dish again until cheese melts.

Yield: Approximately 25 meatballs

One meatball contains:*

Calories	120	Protein	8 g
Carbohydrate	3.5 g	Sodium	312 mg
Total Fat	8 g	Cholesterol	39 mg
		Saturated Fat	3.1 g

** Using ground chuck.*

Tammy Smith
First Place, Main Dishes, 1985

Hot Soya Cinnamon Rolls

DOUGH

1. Dissolve yeast and one tablespoon of sugar in 1 1/2 cups of warm water. Set aside.
2. In large bowl, combine flour, salt, soy flour and nonfat dry milk. Mix well.
3. Add shortening and cut into mixture until the mixture is the consistency of cornmeal.
4. Add yeast mixture and mix well.
5. Cover and let rise until doubled.
6. Knead until smooth and elastic.
7. Roll out on lightly floured surface until 1/2 inch thick.
8. Brush with melted butter.
9. Sprinkle with mixture of cinnamon and 1/2 cup of sugar.
10. Roll into long jelly roll and cut into 1/2-inch-thick slices.
11. Place on lightly greased baking sheet.
12. Let rise until double in size.
13. Bake for 15 to 20 minutes in an oven preheated to 375 degrees F.
14. Glaze while hot.

2 packages yeast
1 tablespoon sugar
1 1/2 cups warm water
3 1/3 cups all-purpose flour
2 teaspoons salt
3/4 cup soy flour
1/2 cup nonfat dry milk
1/2 cup shortening
1/4 cup melted butter
1 1/2 teaspoons cinnamon
1/2 cup sugar

GLAZE

1. Blend ingredients together.
2. Brush Glaze on hot cinnamon rolls.

3 cups confectioners sugar
1/4 cup milk
1/4 cup melted butter

Yield: 36 rolls

One glazed roll has:

Calories	156	Protein	2.6 g
Carbohydrate	24.1 g	Sodium	166 mg
Total Fat	5.7 g	Cholesterol	8 mg
		Saturated Fat	2.1 g

Gloria Freeman
First Place, Coffee Cake Category, 1987

Sour Cream-
Coconut Soya Cake

- 2 cups sugar
- 1 cup butter
- 5 eggs
- 1 teaspoon vanilla extract
- 2 1/4 cups all-purpose flour
- 3/4 cup soy flour
- 1 tablespoon baking powder
- 1 cup soy milk

CAKE

1. Preheat oven to 350 degrees F.
2. Grease 3 nine-inch round cake pans and line bottoms with waxed paper.
3. Cream sugar and butter in large bowl.
4. Add eggs, one at a time, beating well after each.
5. Add vanilla extract. Mix well.
6. Mix all-purpose flour, soy flour, and baking powder.
7. Alternately add flour mixture and soy milk, beginning and ending with flour mixture. Blend batter well after each addition.
8. Pour batter in prepared pans.
9. Bake just until done, 20 to 25 minutes. (If overbaked, cake will be dry and crumbly.)
10. Remove from oven and allow to cool in pans for 5 minutes.
11. Remove layers from pans and allow to cool completely on wire racks.
12. Place Filling between layers and on top of cake.
13. Frost sides and edge of top with cream cheese Frosting.
14. Store tightly covered in the refrigerator. Serve after storing 24 hours.

FILLING

1. In a 2-quart deep bowl, place chilled soy milk.
2. Beat with an electric mixer until thick.
3. Fold in sugar, sour cream and coconut.

1 cup soy milk, chilled

1 cup sugar

1 carton (8 ounces) sour cream

2 packages (7 ounces each) frozen, grated coconut

FROSTING

1. In a one-quart bowl, mix cream cheese and butter until well-blended.
2. Add vanilla extract and confectioners sugar and mix until smooth.

1 package (6 ounces) cream cheese, softened

1/4 cup butter

1 teaspoon vanilla extract

2 cups confectioners sugar

Yield: One 3-layered, 9-inch cake
Makes 24 servings

Each serving contains:
Calories 448
Carbohydrate ...... 47.3 g
Total Fat .... 27.5 g
Protein .... 6.3 g
Sodium .... 196 mg
Cholesterol .... 96 mg
Saturated Fat ..... 18.6 g

Laurie Stutson
First Place, Cakes, 1987
Best Overall Winner, 1987

Tony Q CHAMPAGNE

Frog Festival Has Rayne Hopping!

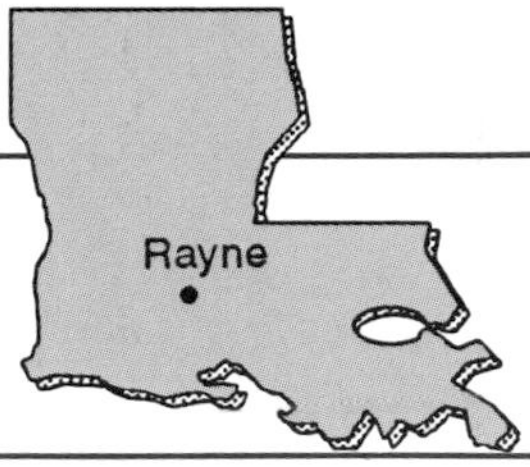

Rayne

The humble frog goes from the bayou to center stage in Rayne every September at the Frog Festival.

In the past, Rayne was the home of a thriving industry that involved catching and shipping giant bullfrogs all over the world. The rice fields, bayous and irrigation ditches surrounding this southwest Louisiana town were the perfect homes for the amphibians.

Ironically, the Frog Festival, which began in 1972, came at the end of the frog industry.

Touted as "pure Cajun fun for the whole family," the Frog Festival features a wide variety of live musical entertainment, a street fair and a great variety of foods, including frog legs, fried alligator and crawfish pie.

But, this festival wouldn't be complete without frogs starring in several major roles. There's frog racing and jumping, a frog leg eating contest and, one of the most popular events, a Frog Derby, where costumed frogs leap for the finish line.

Royalty is an important part of the festival, and kings and queens of many ages are crowned. There's a diaper derby, a Little Tadpole contest and, of course, a cooking competition.

The Frog Festival is held annually on the second weekend in September and is sponsored by the Rayne Chamber of Commerce. Watch for the welcoming mural of frogs as you leave I-10 and arrive in Rayne.

Crispy Frog Legs

- 6 pair of frog legs
- 3/4 cup lemon juice or vinegar
- Crushed ice
- 1/2 cup milk
- 3 eggs, separated
- 1 tablespoon Lou Ana Vegetable Oil
- 1/8 teaspoon salt
- Salt and pepper, for frog legs, if desired
- 3/4 cup all-purpose flour
- Lou Ana Vegetable Oil for frying

1. Wash frog legs thoroughly.
2. Place in large bowl, sprinkle with lemon juice or vinegar, and cover with ice.
3. Refrigerate 1 to 3 hours.
4. In a 2-quart bowl, combine milk, egg yolks, one tablespoon of Lou Ana Vegetable Oil, and 1/8 teaspoon of salt; mix well.
5. Beat egg whites until stiff; fold into batter.
6. Sprinkle frog legs with salt and pepper, if desired.
7. Dip each frog leg in batter and dredge in flour.
8. Fry until golden brown in Lou Ana Vegetable Oil heated to 375 degrees F.
9. Drain on paper towels.

Yield: 6 servings (2 frog legs per serving)

Each serving contains:

Calories	305	Protein	20.7 g
Carbohydrate	2 g	Sodium	14 mg
Total Fat	23.7 g	Cholesterol	20 mg
		Saturated Fat	5.9 g

Antonia Hoffpauir

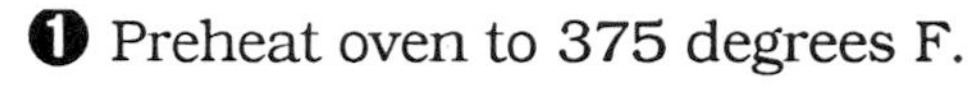

Stuffed Frog Legs

- 12 large frog legs
- 1 1/2 tablespoons butter
- 3/4 cup chopped onion
- 1/8 cup chopped green bell pepper
- 1/8 cup chopped celery
- 1 cup fresh clean shrimp, ground or chopped fine
- 1/2 cup fresh crabmeat
- 3/4 cup cooked rice
- 1/8 teaspoon Tabasco sauce
- 1/2 teaspoon Creole seasoning
- 1/2 can (10.5-ounce size) oyster soup
- Milk for dipping
- Lou Ana Fish Fry for coating

1. Preheat oven to 375 degrees F.
2. Make pockets in largest part of frog legs, then set aside.
3. Melt butter; add onion, green bell pepper and celery. Sauté until brown.
4. Add shrimp and crabmeat. Simmer about 30 minutes.
5. Add rice and mix well. Season with Tabasco sauce and Creole seasoning.
6. Add soup as needed to moisten.
7. Stuff mixture into frog legs.
8. Dip stuffed frog legs into milk and coat with Lou Ana Fish Fry.
9. Arrange in shallow pan and bake for 40 to 45 minutes.

Yield: 12 stuffed frog legs

One frog leg has:

Calories	132	Protein	16.2 g
Carbohydrate	10.8 g	Sodium	577 mg
Total Fat	3.3 g	Cholesterol	40 mg
		Saturated Fat	1.2 g

Josette H. Habetz

TONY Q. CHAMPAGNE

Watermelon Cookies, Anyone?

Franklinton

Sitting on the back porch on a sultry summer evening eating watermelon and spitting the slippery black seeds into the grass is a Southern tradition that's right at home at the Washington Parish Watermelon Festival.

This south Louisiana parish is known for its sweet watermelons, and this annual festival draws attention to this king of melons at the height of its season.

Held on the second weekend in July in Franklinton, the festival began in 1985 as a means to promote the local watermelon and vegetable industry and to raise money for a farmer's market.

The watermelon seed-spitting contest is one of the funniest attractions at the festival. Contestants find that it's one thing to spit a seed at home and another to have a mouthful of seeds in front of a crowd of laughing onlookers.

One contestant lost his dentures as well as his seeds when he spit, a festival organizer recalls.

The festival record for seed-spitting is 35 feet. That's 30 feet short of the Guinness Book of World Records, but festival planners say they will witness any attempt to set a world record.

There's also a watermelon auction, where prize watermelons are auctioned off.

There are more ways to eat a watermelon than fresh from the vine. The 1989 festival catalog featured recipes for watermelon divinity, watermelon punch, pizza, ambrosia, pickles, ice cream and even cookies.

Festival highlights include a fireworks display, as well as the usual midway, carnival rides and beauty queen contest. There is also live music, an antique car show and a rodeo.

Watermelon Rind Preserves

Watermelon(s)

Salt

Water

Ground ginger

Sugar

Lemon(s), sliced and seeds removed

1. Peel off all the green portion of the outer rind of the watermelon(s) and all red melon, leaving only the white rind. Cut into strips about 1/2- to 3/4-inch thick. Measure in quarts. Soak in cold salt water about 6 hours or overnight. For salt solution, use 1/2 cup of salt to 1 gallon of water.

2. Drain, rinse in cold water, and drain again. Mix 2 teaspoons of ground ginger in each quart of water and barely cover melon rind. Cook until "fork tender" (about 10 to 12 minutes). Do not overcook.

3. For each 2 quarts of raw, prepared rind, make a syrup using 5 cups of sugar, 3 cups of water, and 1 lemon. Boil syrup 5 minutes; add pre-cooked rind and boil gently until preserves are clear and translucent (about 1 1/4 hours). If syrup becomes too thick before rind is clear, thin by adding a small amount of boiling water.

4. Fill hot, sterilized jars with preserves and syrup to within 1/2 inch of the top. Remove air bubbles, wipe sealing edge clean, and put on new lids prepared according to manufacturer's instructions. Seal and process for 10 minutes in a boiling water canner.

Variation: For a great flavor, but darker color, use cinnamon and cloves instead of ginger. Use the above proportions with these modifications: Precook in clear water (no ginger). To syrup, add 2 sticks of cinnamon and 1 teaspoon of whole cloves tied in a thin white cloth bag. Remove spice bag before filling jars.

Louisiana Cooperative Extension Service
Louisiana State University, Baton Rouge

Watermelon Rind Preserve Cookies

1 cup butter

1/8 teaspoon salt

1/2 cup sugar

1/4 teaspoon grated lemon rind

2 egg yolks

2 3/4 cups sifted cake flour

1/2 cup Watermelon Rind Preserves (Recipe on facing page)

1. Preheat oven to 350 degrees F.
2. In bowl of a stand mixer, cream butter.
3. Add salt, sugar, and lemon rind. Mix well.
4. Add egg yolks. Mix well.
5. Set mixer on low speed and add cake flour. Mix well.
6. Shape pieces of dough into balls about one inch in diameter.
7. Place balls of dough one inch apart on an ungreased baking sheet.
8. Use index finger to make a shallow depression in top of each cookie.
9. Place about 1/4 teaspoon of preserves in depression of each cookie.
10. Bake for approximately 12 minutes or until lightly browned.
11. Remove baked cookies from cookie sheet and place on rack to cool.

Yield: 3 dozen cookies

Each cookie contains:

Calories 93
Carbohydrate ...... 10.5 g
Total Fat .... 5.5 g
Protein .... 0.8 g
Sodium .... 62 mg
Cholesterol .... 29 mg
Saturated Fat .... 3.3 g

Watermelon Preserve Cake

- 1 cup butter
- 2 cups sugar
- 4 eggs
- 3 cups all-purpose flour
- 1/2 teaspoon baking soda
- 1 teaspoon cinnamon
- 1/2 teaspoon cloves
- 1 cup buttermilk
- 1 teaspoon vanilla extract
- 1 cup Watermelon Rind Preserves (Recipe on page 140.)
- 1 cup pecans, chopped

1. Preheat oven to 325 degrees F.
2. Grease and flour 10-cup bundt cake pan.
3. In bowl of a stand mixer, cream butter and sugar until light and fluffy.
4. Add eggs, one at a time, beating well after each addition.
5. Mix flour, soda, and spices in a one-quart bowl.
6. Add flour mixture alternately with buttermilk to creamed mixture.
7. Fold in vanilla, preserves, and nuts.
8. Pour into prepared bundt pan.
9. Bake 1 to 1 1/2 hours in preheated oven.
10. Cool in pan 15 minutes.
11. Remove from pan.

Makes 24 slices

Each slice contains:

Calories	267	Protein	3.3 g
Carbohydrate	37.9 g	Sodium	119 mg
Total Fat	12 g	Cholesterol	67 mg
		Saturated Fat	5.4 g

Watermelon Punch

1. Scoop out melon from rind and remove seeds.
2. Blend melon. Measure, then add reconstituted lemonade, blended strawberries, and sugar.
3. Blend again.
4. Chill.
5. Add ginger ale, if desired, before serving.

Note: May use watermelon rind as punch bowl.

10 cups watermelon, blended

12 cups reconstituted lemonade

4 cups frozen unsweetened strawberries (blended)

1/2 cup sugar

Ginger ale (optional)

Yield: 28 cups
Makes 56 servings (1/2 cup each)

Each serving contains:

Calories	47	Protein	0.5 g
Carbohydrate	11.5 g	Sodium	2 mg
Total Fat	0.2 g	Cholesterol	0 mg
		Saturated Fat	0 g

Summer Salad

1. Combine fruits.
2. Pour orange juice over fruit and mix well.
3. Chill and serve.

1/2 cup mandarin orange slices

1/2 cup watermelon cubes

1/2 cup cantaloupe cubes

1/2 cup white grapes

1/2 cup pineapple chunks

1/2 cup cold orange juice

Yield: 2 1/2 cups
Makes 5 servings (1/2 cup each)

Each serving contains:

Calories	63	Protein	0.8 g
Carbohydrate	15.9 g	Sodium	4 mg
Total Fat	0.3 g	Cholesterol	0 mg
		Saturated Fat	0 g

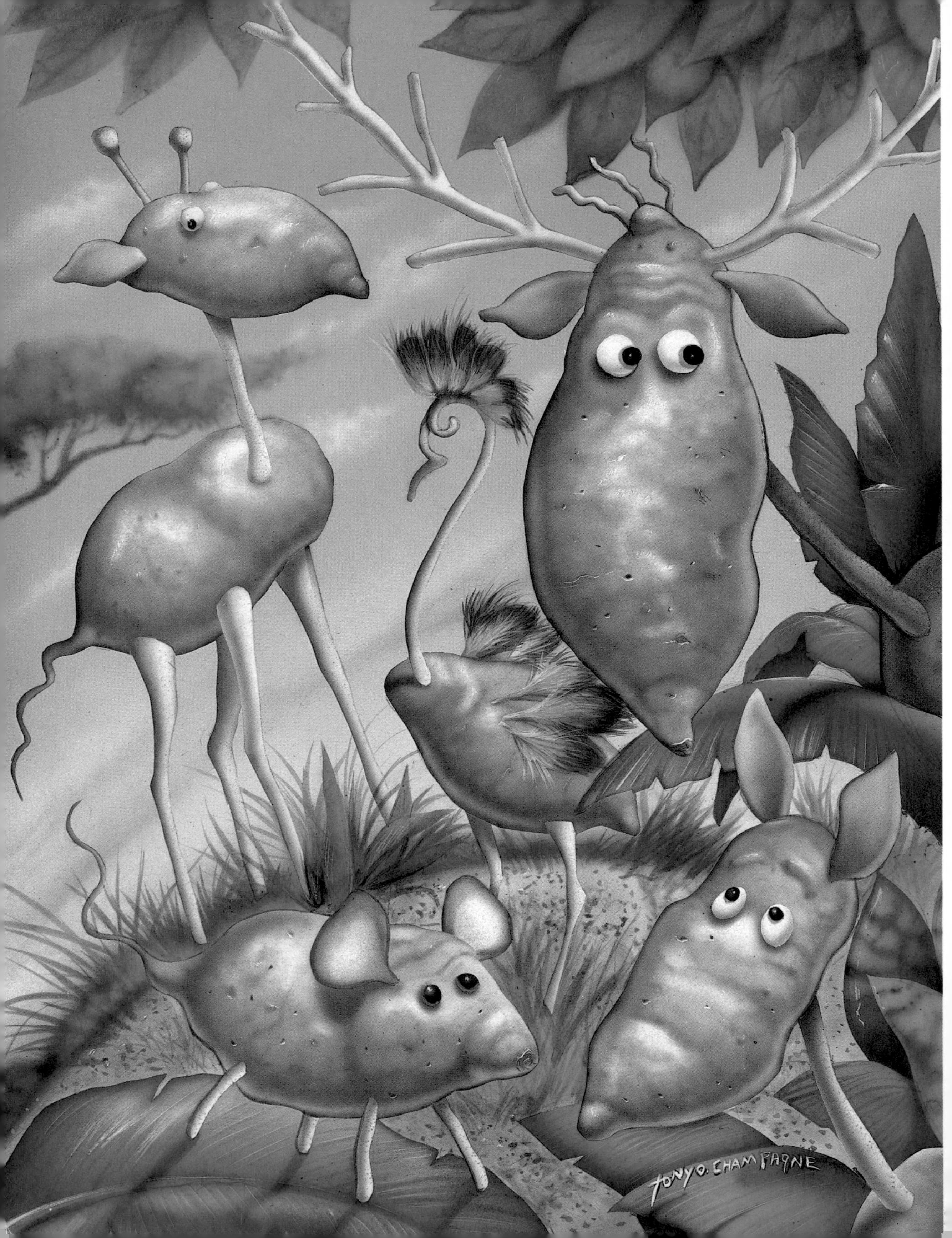
TONY O. CHAMPAGNE

Delicious, Nutritious Yam Draws 150,000 to Opelousas

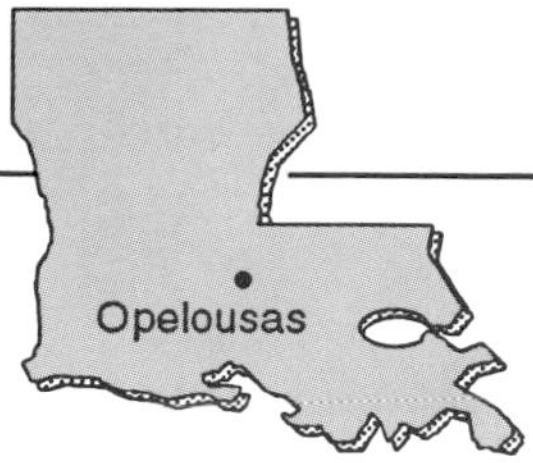

Opelousas

Back in 1946 the promoters of the festival recognizing the golden Louisiana yam were determined to call attention to the yam in every way imaginable.

Because of that, they didn't name it the Yam Festival, but the Yambilee.

When they built an auditorium for the festival, it was naturally called the "Yamatorium."

The parade was named the "Grand Louisyam Parade," and the singing group, of course, would be the "Yamettes."

Perhaps the most unique idea of all was the creation of "Yamimals," which are curiously shaped yams dressed like little animals, using pipe cleaners, feathers, construction paper or Play Dough.

Indeed, the Yamimal competition, with four divisions ranging from children to senior citizens, is one of this festival's most unique attractions.

Other highlights of the Yambilee, which is held each October in Opelousas, are a carnival, parade, talent contest, beauty contests and a yam cooking contest. Past winners have included yam pie, yam and shrimp appetizers and yam cookies.

The Yambilee owes its beginning to J.W. Low, a native Texan, who adopted Opelousas as his home. Over a cup of coffee, he suggested to his friend, Felix Dezauche, a yam shipper involved in every phase of the yam industry, that a festival be started to promote the yam. Today the Yambilee is one of the state's largest festivals, attracting some 150,000 to Opelousas, the parish seat of St. Landry Parish.

Yam & Crabmeat Au Gratin

- 4 tablespoons butter, divided
- 1 cup chopped onion
- 2 tablespoons chopped green bell pepper
- 2 tablespoons all-purpose flour
- 1 cup milk
- 3 slices American cheese
- 1/2 cup crabmeat
- 3/4 cup mashed yams
- 1/2 teaspoon Creole seasoning
- 1/2 cup breadcrumbs

1. Preheat oven to 350 degrees F.
2. Grease a one-quart casserole dish.
3. Place 2 tablespoons of butter in an 8" skillet.
4. Melt butter. Add onion and green bell pepper. Sauté until limp, but not brown.
5. Stir flour into the cooked vegetables and heat until bubbly.
6. Slowly add milk, stirring constantly. Continue heating until thick.
7. Add cheese slices, crabmeat, yams, and Creole seasoning. Adjust seasoning, if desired.
8. Pour into prepared casserole dish.
9. Melt the remaining 2 tablespoons of butter and mix with the breadcrumbs.
10. Sprinkle breadcrumbs over crab mixture.
11. Place in preheated oven and bake for 30 minutes.

Yield: 2 1/2 cups
Makes 5 servings (1/2 cup each)

Each serving contains:
Calories 252
Carbohydrate ...... 25.2 g
Total Fat .... 12.4 g
Protein .... 10.2 g
Sodium .... 404 mg
Cholesterol .... 49 mg
Saturated Fat .... 7.4 g

Yam & Shrimp Hors D'Oeuvres

CRUST

- 1/2 cup butter
- 3 ounces cream cheese
- 1 cup all-purpose flour

1. Preheat oven to 450 degrees F.
2. Blend butter and cream cheese.
3. Stir in flour.
4. Shape into 36 balls about one inch in diameter.
5. Press small amounts of dough into party-size muffin pans.
6. Press sides and bottom with fork.

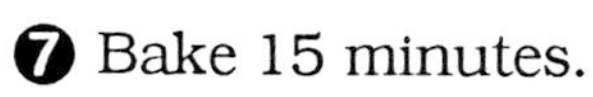

7. Bake 15 minutes.

FILLING

- 1/4 cup finely chopped onion
- 1 tablespoon green bell pepper
- 2 tablespoons butter
- 1 cup shrimp, peeled and chopped
- 1 tablespoon parsley
- 1 cup cooked, mashed yams
- 1/2 teaspoon salt
- 1/4 teaspoon red pepper

1. Sauté onion and green bell pepper in butter.
2. Add shrimp and parsley. Cook until shrimp is done (about 5 minutes).
3. Remove from heat and stir in yams and seasonings.
4. Fill pie shells.

Yield: 36 hors d'oeuvres

Each hors d'oeuvre has:

Calories	49	Protein	1.7 g
Carbohydrate	3.6 g	Sodium	72 mg
Total Fat	3.2 g	Cholesterol	17 mg
		Saturated Fat	1.9 g

Yam Casserole

CASSEROLE

- 3 cups cooked, mashed yams
- 1/2 cup sugar
- 2 eggs
- 1 teaspoon vanilla extract
- 1/3 cup milk
- 1/2 cup butter

TOPPING

- 1/2 cup firmly packed brown sugar
- 3/4 cup all-purpose flour
- 1/4 cup butter
- 1/2 cup pecans

1. Preheat oven to 350 degrees F.
2. In a 2-quart bowl combine yams, sugar, eggs, vanilla, milk and 1/2 cup of butter.
3. Beat with electric mixer until smooth.
4. Spoon into a greased 2-quart casserole dish.
5. In a 1-quart bowl prepare Topping: Combine brown sugar and flour; cut butter into mixture; add pecans.
6. Sprinkle Topping over yam mixture.
7. Bake for 30 minutes.

Yield: 5 cups
Makes 10 servings (1/2 cup each)

Each serving contains:
Calories 364
Carbohydrate ...... 45.1 g
Total Fat .... 19.1 g
Protein .... 4 g
Sodium .... 171 mg
Cholesterol .... 93 mg
Saturated Fat .... 9.4 g

Jo LaCaze

French Fried Golden Louisiana Yams

1. Wash and peel the Louisiana yams.
2. Cut peeled yams into strips suitable for deep fat frying.
3. Mix salt and ice water. Add strips to salt water.
4. Soak strips in salted water about ten minutes.
5. Drain and then dry between absorbent paper towels.
6. Preheat Lou Ana Vegetable Oil to 365 degrees F.
7. Add strips of yams and fry until brown.
8. Drain well on absorbent paper.
9. Sprinkle with confectioner's sugar or salt, if desired.

Makes 4 servings

Each serving contains:
Calories 138
Carbohydrate ...... 26.3 g
Total Fat .... 2.9 g
Protein .... 1.9 g
Sodium .... 193 mg
Cholesterol .... 0 mg
Saturated Fat .... 0.7 g

Janel Duplechain

3 golden Louisiana yams

1 tablespoon salt

3 cups ice water

Lou Ana Vegetable Oil for frying

Confectioners sugar to taste

Yam-Sherry Casserole

6 cups cooked yams, sliced

1 tablespoon grated orange

1/3 cup cooking sherry (bourbon may be used)

1/2 cup orange juice

1/2 cup brown sugar

1 teaspoon salt

1/4 cup of butter

1. Preheat oven to 350 degrees F.
2. Butter bottom and sides of a 9" x 13" x 2" casserole dish.
3. Place sliced yams in casserole dish (1 layer thick).
4. Mix grated orange, sherry, and orange juice. Pour over sliced yams.
5. Mix sugar and salt. Sprinkle over yams.
6. Cut butter into small pieces and distribute evenly over yams.
7. Cover and bake for 45 to 50 minutes until almost all the juice (about 1/4 cup remaining) has cooked into the yams.
8. Remove from oven and serve.

Makes 10 servings

Each serving contains:
Calories 243
Carbohydrate .... 46 g
Total Fat ....5.1 g
Protein .... 2.5 g
Sodium .... 301 mg
Cholesterol .... 12 mg
Saturated Fat .... 2.9 g

Mrs. Daniel Mestayer

Sweet Potato Pie

1. Preheat oven to 375 degrees F.
2. Blend potatoes, butter, and sugar.
3. Add eggs one at a time, beating well after each egg.
4. Add vanilla extract, spices, salt, and milk. Mix well.
5. Pour in unbaked pie shell.
6. Place in preheated oven and bake for 35 minutes or until set.
7. Remove from oven and cool.
8. Store in refrigerator.
9. Serve with whipped topping, if desired.

Yield: One 9-inch pie
Makes 8 servings

Each serving contains:

Calories	413	Protein	5.3 g
Carbohydrate	52.6 g	Sodium	256 mg
Total Fat	21.3 g	Cholesterol	148 mg
		Saturated Fat	8.4 g

Cedric L. Johnson

2 cups mashed sweet potatoes

1/2 cup butter

1 cup sugar

2 eggs

1 teaspoon vanilla extract

1/4 teaspoon nutmeg

1/8 teaspoon cloves

1/4 teaspoon cinnamon

1/8 teaspoon salt

1 cup milk

1 9-inch unbaked pie shell

Yam Muffins

2 cups all-purpose flour

1 tablespoon baking powder

1/2 teaspoon salt

1 tablespoon cinnamon

1/2 teaspoon ground nutmeg

1/2 teaspoon ground cloves

2 cups sugar

1 egg, beaten

1 1/2 tablespoons Lou Ana Vegetable Oil

1/3 cup milk

1 cup mashed sweet potatoes

MUFFINS

1. Grease 18 muffin cups.
2. Preheat oven to 375 degrees F.
3. In a 2-quart bowl, mix together flour, baking powder, salt, cinnamon, nutmeg, cloves, and sugar. Set aside.
4. In a 1-quart bowl, combine beaten egg, Lou Ana Vegetable Oil and milk. Mix well.
5. Add mashed yams to egg mixture and mix well.
6. Add liquid mixture to dry ingredients and stir only until all dry ingredients are moist. Do not overmix.
7. Fill greased muffin cups 2/3 full.
8. Place in preheated oven and bake for 20 to 25 minutes. Cool.
9. Frost with cream cheese frosting, if desired.

4 ounces cream cheese, softened

1 tablespoon butter

1 teaspoon vanilla extract

2 1/4 cups confectioners sugar

FROSTING

1. Place cream cheese and butter in a 2-quart bowl and cream well.
2. Add vanilla extract. Mix well.
3. Add confectioners sugar and cream well.

Yield: 18 muffins
Makes 18 servings

One frosted muffin has:

Calories	252	Protein	2.6 g
Carbohydrate	51 g	Sodium	131 mg
Total Fat	4.8 g	Cholesterol	24 mg
		Saturated Fat	2.3 g

Yam Cookies

COOKIES

- 1 cup shortening
- 1 cup sugar
- 1 egg
- 1 cup canned yams (mashed)
- 1 teaspoon cinnamon
- 1/2 teaspoon ginger
- 1/2 teaspoon salt
- 2 cups all-purpose flour
- 1 teaspoon baking powder
- 1 cup chopped dates
- 1/2 cup chopped nuts

1. Preheat oven to 350 degrees F.
2. Place shortening and sugar in a 2-quart mixing bowl and cream until light and fluffy.
3. Add egg and beat well.
4. Add yams and mix well.

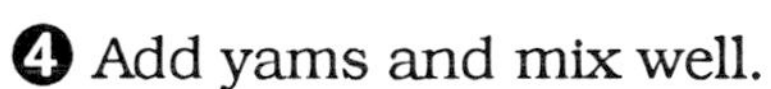

5. Combine cinnamon, ginger, salt, flour, and baking powder. Add to creamed mixture. Mix well.
6. Stir in dates and nuts.
7. Drop by the teaspoonful about 2 inches apart onto a greased cookie sheet. Flour fingertips lightly and pat the top of each cookie to flatten slightly.
8. Bake for 15 minutes or until golden brown.
9. If desired, drizzle with Brown Sugar Glaze while warm.

BROWN SUGAR GLAZE

- 1/4 cup brown sugar
- 2 tablespoons all-purpose flour
- 5 tablespoons milk
- 3 tablespoons melted butter
- 1 cup confectioners sugar
- 1/2 teaspoon vanilla extract

1. Combine brown sugar, flour, milk and butter in a heavy saucepan and bring to a boil.
2. Cook 2 minutes.
3. Remove from heat and stir until partly cool.
4. Add confectioners sugar and vanilla extract. Beat until smooth.
5. Drizzle over warm cookies.

Yield: 6 dozen cookies

One glazed cookie has:

Calories	81	Protein	0.7 g
Carbohydrate	11.2 g	Sodium	31 mg
Total Fat	4 g	Cholesterol	5 mg
		Saturated Fat	0.8 g

Yam Cake

CAKE

- 1 box yellow cake mix that requires addition of butter
- 1 cup water
- 1/2 cup butter, softened
- 3 eggs

1. Preheat oven to 350 degrees F. Grease bottoms of two 8-inch cake pans. Line bottoms with waxed paper.
2. Put cake mix, water, butter, and eggs in a 2-quart mixing bowl.
3. Mix at low speed of mixer until ingredients are blended.
4. Beat at high speed of mixer for 2 minutes.
5. Pour batter into prepared pans and bake 25 minutes.
6. Allow cake to cool in pans for 5 minutes.
7. Remove from pans and allow cake to completely cool on wire racks.
8. Place Filling between the layers and on the top layer.

FILLING

- 1 1/2 cups sweet potatoes, cooked
- 1/4 cup butter, softened
- 1/2 cup sugar
- 1 teaspoon vanilla extract
- 1/2 teaspoon nutmeg
- 1/2 cup chopped nuts

1. Mash cooked sweet potatoes. Set aside.
2. In a 2-quart bowl, cream butter.
3. Add sugar and cream well.
4. Add mashed sweet potatoes, vanilla extract, and nutmeg.
5. Beat until well-blended.
6. Stir in chopped nuts.

Note: If mixture is too thick to spread, add cream, one tablespoon at a time, until mixture is of spreading consistency.

Yield: One 8-inch, 2-layer cake
Makes 20 servings

Each serving contains:

Calories	236	Protein	2.8 g
Carbohydrate	27.5 g	Sodium	242 mg
Total Fat	13.1 g	Cholesterol	75 mg
		Saturated Fat	6.4 g

Katina Fuselier

Yam Cheese Cake

CRUST

- 1 2/3 cups graham cracker crumbs
- 1/4 cup butter
- 1/4 cup sugar

1. Preheat oven to 350 degrees F.
2. Mix graham cracker crumbs, butter, and sugar in food processor.
3. Press into bottom of 9" x 13" x 2" baking dish.
4. Bake at 350 degrees F. for 10 minutes. Remove from oven and set aside to cool.

FILLING

- 1 envelope unflavored gelatin
- 1/4 cup water
- 2 packages (8-ounce size) cream cheese, softened
- 3 cups mashed yams
- 2 eggs, beaten
- 1 1/2 cups sugar
- 1 1/2 cups butter, softened
- 2 teaspoons vanilla extract

1. Combine gelatin and water in a small bowl or cup. Allow gelatin to hydrate.
2. In a one-quart bowl, beat cream cheese with mixer until smooth and no lumps are present. Set aside.
3. In a two-quart sauce pan, mix mashed yams, eggs, sugar, and butter with mixer.
4. Heat over medium heat, stirring constantly, until mixture is hot throughout.
5. Add hydrated gelatin and stir until gelatin dissolves.
6. Remove from heat.
7. Fold in beaten cream cheese and add vanilla extract. Blend well.
8. Pour into 9" x 13" x 2" baking dish lined with graham cracker crust.
9. Chill 3 hours or until firm.
10. Cut into 20 pieces approximately 2" x 2 1/2".

Makes 20 servings (2" x 2 1/2")

One serving contains:

Calories	271	Protein	3.6 g
Carbohydrate	29.3 g	Sodium	194 mg
Total Fat	15.9 g	Cholesterol	71 mg
		Saturated Fat	9.6 g

Yam Parfait

1 cup all-purpose flour

1/2 cup butter

1 cup chopped nuts

FIRST LAYER

Mix together ingredients and press in bottom of 9" x 13" x 2" pan. Bake in 350 degree F. oven for 20 minutes. Cool thoroughly.

1 package (8 ounces) cream cheese, softened

1 cup confectioners sugar

1 cup whipped topping

SECOND LAYER

Whip cream cheese and confectioners sugar together until light and fluffy. Fold in whipped topping. Spread over crust. Cool.

2 cups cooked yams, mashed

1/4 cup sugar

1 teaspoon vanilla extract

THIRD LAYER

Combine yams, sugar, and flavoring. Beat well. Spread over cream cheese layer.

2 tablespoons cornstarch

1/4 cup sugar

1 can (12 ounces) crushed pineapple

FOURTH LAYER

In a one-quart saucepan, mix cornstarch and sugar together. Add crushed pineapple. Stir until mixture is well-blended. Heat over medium heat, stirring constantly until thickened. Cool. Spread over yam layer.

FIFTH LAYER

Prepare, according to directions on package of pudding mix. Spread over pineapple layer.

1 package (3 1/2 ounces) instant vanilla pudding mix

2 cups cold milk

SIXTH LAYER

Before serving, cover top with whipped topping. Sprinkle with pecans to garnish. Cut into pieces 2" x 2 1/2".

2 cups whipped topping

1/2 cup pecans, chopped

Makes 20 servings

Each serving contains:

Calories	300	Protein	3.6 g
Carbohydrate	35.1 g	Sodium	115 mg
Total Fat	17.1 g	Cholesterol	29 mg
		Saturated Fat	8.3 g

Rosetta Bordelon

TONY O. CHAMPAGNE

The *Boucherie*: An Old French Custom Continues

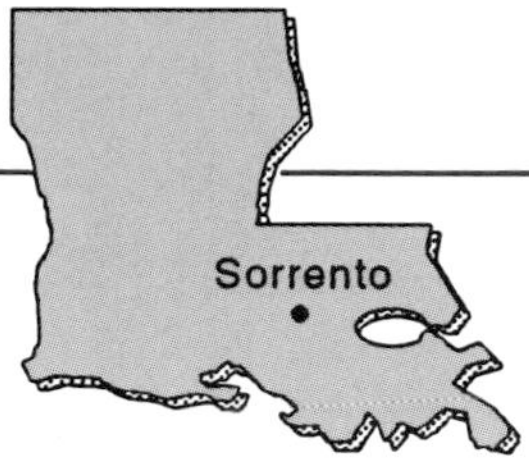

Sorrento

The *boucherie*, or hog butchering, is a south Louisiana tradition started by the early French settlers. During the fall and winter, families and friends would gather and butcher a hog, then divide the meat among the participants. The *boucheries* continued throughout the cold weather, thus ensuring fresh meat for everyone.

It is this spirit of friendship and work, combined with good food, that the Sorrento *Boucherie* Festival strives to preserve.

The festival, which is held on the grounds of the Ascension Parish Civic Center on the second full weekend in October, had its beginning back in the 1960s, when a former Sorrento mayor annually invited townspeople to his hunting camp for a *boucherie*.

The Sorrento Lions Club began the festival, as it is known today, in 1978. Festival proceeds go to Lions Club projects such as providing eyeglasses, hearing aids and summer camp for handicapped children.

Although an actual butchering doesn't take place during the festival, a cracklin-cooking contest does, and cracklin-making is an important ingredient of a *boucherie*. Cracklins are made from cubes of pork fat that are fried for several hours in huge cast iron pots.

The preliminary cracklin contest is on Saturday and the Cracklin Cooking World Champion is crowned on Sunday after a final round of competition. Yes, the cracklins are sold to hungry festival-goers.

Other pork specialities are available to eat all weekend. Jambalaya, hogshead cheese and boudin are also on the menu, as well as tamer hot dogs and hamburgers.

No south Louisiana festival is complete without a parade, plenty of Cajun and country bands to provide dance music and a beauty contest. The Sorrento *Boucherie* Festival has those, plus a carnival midway.

Boudin

- 3 cups water
- 1/2 pound boneless pork, cubed
- 1/8 pound pork liver
- 1/2 cup chopped onion
- 1/4 cup chopped green onion
- 1 teaspoon parsley flakes
- 1 teaspoon celery flakes
- 3/4 teaspoon salt
- 1/2 teaspoon black pepper
- 3/4 teaspoon red pepper
- 3/4 cup cooked rice
- Sausage casings

1. Place water, boneless pork, and pork liver in a 2-quart saucepan. Bring mixture to a boil over high heat.
2. Reduce to a medium heat setting and simmer until pork is tender.
3. Remove pork and liver from stock.
4. Grind pork and liver (may use food processor, if desired).
5. Add onion, green onion, and other seasonings to stock. Cook until onions are tender.
6. Add ground meat to vegetable-stock mixture. Cook until most of the water has evaporated.
7. Stir in cooked rice. Adjust seasonings, if desired.
8. Stuff rice-meat mixture into sausage casings.
9. Prick casings 3 to 4 times each to prevent bursting during cooking.
10. Cook boudin in simmering water for 12 minutes. Remove from water and serve.

Yield: Two links, each approximately 9 inches long
Serves six 3-inch pieces

Each 3-inch piece has:

Calories	154	Protein	9.5 g
Carbohydrate	7.4 g	Sodium	428 mg
Total Fat	9.3 g	Cholesterol	58 mg
		Saturated Fat	3.3 g

Hog Head Cheese

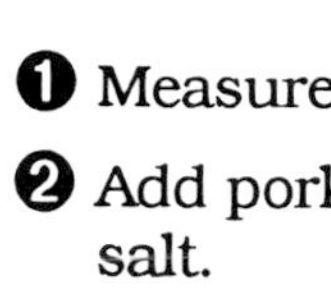

- 10 cups water
- 2 1/2 pounds pork meat
- 1 pig's foot
- 2 teaspoons salt, divided
- 3/4 pound onions, chopped
- 1 tablespoon parsley flakes
- 1 tablespoon celery flakes
- 1 cup chopped green onion
- 1 teaspoon black pepper
- 3/4 teaspoon red pepper

1. Measure water into a 5-quart saucepot.
2. Add pork meat, pig's foot, and one teaspoon salt.
3. Cook until meat is tender and pig's foot can be easily deboned. Approximately 3 cups of liquid should remain in saucepot.
4. Add chopped onions, parsley flakes, celery flakes, chopped green onions, the remaining teaspoon of salt, black pepper, and red pepper. Cook about 3 minutes.
5. Remove meat from liquid. Reserve liquid.
6. Debone meat.
7. Place meat in food processor bowl. Chop well, but do not puree.
8. Mix chopped ingredients and reserved liquid.
9. Pour into a 9" x 13" x 2" pan.
10. Chill thoroughly.

Yield: one 9" x 13" x 2" pan
Makes 60 servings (2 tablespoons each)

Each serving contains:

Calories	75	Protein	4.9 g
Carbohydrate	0.5 g	Sodium	94 mg
Total Fat	5.7 g	Cholesterol	22 mg
		Saturated Fat	2 g

Tony O. CHAMPAGNE

Big Name Entertainers Draw Crowds to Bayou Lacombe

Lacombe

The Bayou Lacombe Crab Fest, held every June, was created in 1977 to help put this small town on the map and to raise money for charitable causes.

The strategy has worked because this community, located across Lake Pontchartrain from New Orleans, has created a small town event with top name entertainment and delicious food. The festival has used its proceeds to benefit various philanthropic endeavors, such as Children's Hospital in New Orleans and St. Jude's in Memphis.

Modeled after the highly successful New Orleans Jazz and Heritage Festival, the festival has brought such stars as Irma Thomas to Bayou Lacombe to perform for the 40,000 festival-goers who attend annually.

In addition to big name performers, local music groups are invited to perform on another stage, where the possibility of being discovered by a record company scout increases the desire to participate.

While the focus is on food and music, there are other activities as well. The Mitchell Brothers' Show offers amusement rides and side shows. On Sunday afternoon, contests for children, such as watermelon-eating and bubble gum-chewing, are held.

As is the tradition at many festivals, a king and queen are selected annually, and the queen is sent to the Washington, D.C., Mardi Gras Ball to represent the Crab Festival.

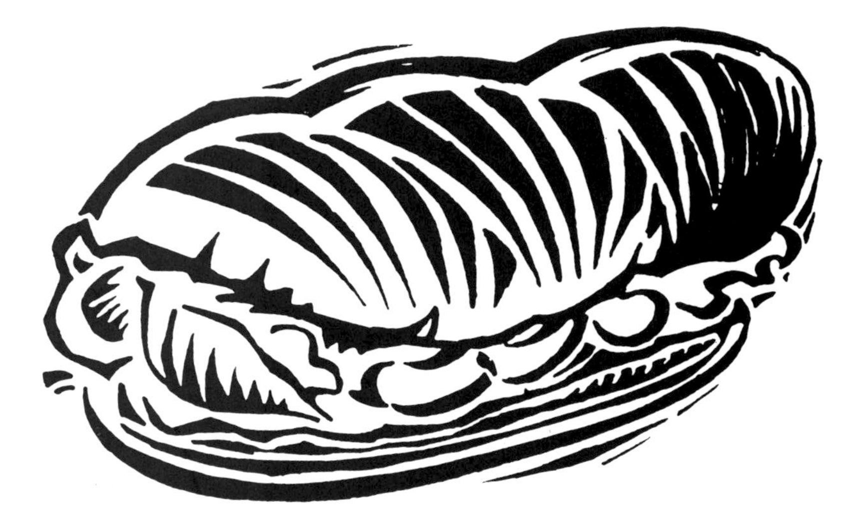

The New Orleans Fried Soft-Shell Crab Po-Boy

Soft-shell crabs

1 cup milk

1 egg

1 package (12 ounces) Lou Ana Fish Fry Mix

Lou Ana Corn Oil for frying, preheated

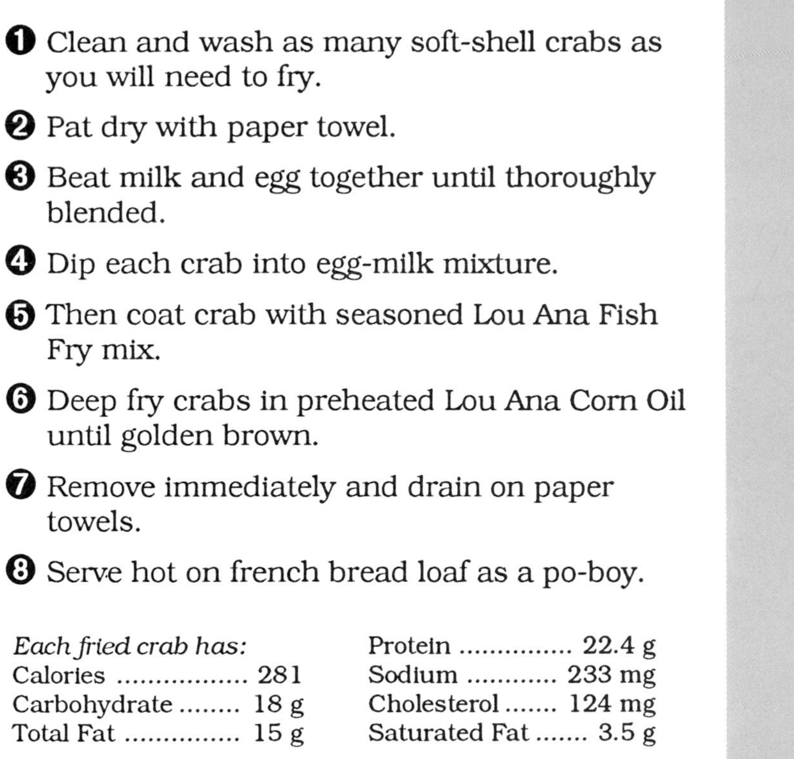

❶ Clean and wash as many soft-shell crabs as you will need to fry.

❷ Pat dry with paper towel.

❸ Beat milk and egg together until thoroughly blended.

❹ Dip each crab into egg-milk mixture.

❺ Then coat crab with seasoned Lou Ana Fish Fry mix.

❻ Deep fry crabs in preheated Lou Ana Corn Oil until golden brown.

❼ Remove immediately and drain on paper towels.

❽ Serve hot on french bread loaf as a po-boy.

Each fried crab has:

Calories	281	Protein	22.4 g
Carbohydrate	18 g	Sodium	233 mg
Total Fat	15 g	Cholesterol	124 mg
		Saturated Fat	3.5 g

Official Recipe of the Bayou Lacombe Crab Festival

The Good Times Roll in Breaux Bridge Each May

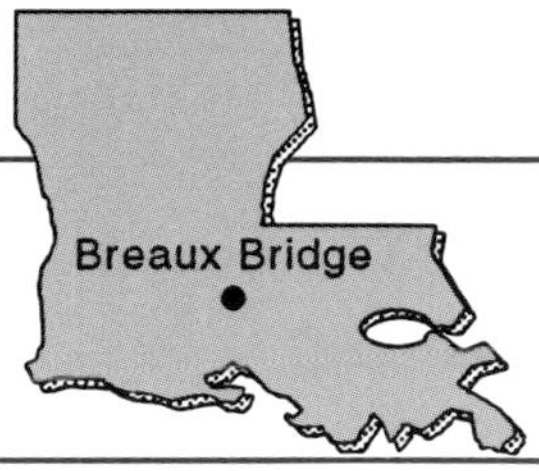

Breaux Bridge

Spring in south Louisiana is crawfish season, and the first weekend in May is the time for a crustacean celebration at the Crawfish Festival in Breaux Bridge.

First held in 1959, the festival was an instant success. Over the years it has evolved into two events held on the same weekend.

At *Parc Hardy*, family-oriented events are scheduled, including a *fais-do-do* (Cajun dance), crawfish races, crawfish-cooking contest and native craft exhibitions. Other special features of the festival include a story-telling pavilion, a folklore pavilion and a *bourée* (card game) exhibition.

Downtown, where the festival takes to the streets, a free spirited, Mardi Gras atmosphere reigns. Large quantities of beer and other spirits are consumed, and party-goers dance to bands playing on several street corners.

One of the festival highlights is the parade, which includes local beauties, floats depicting Cajun culture and history, marching bands and costumed performers. No matter where festival-goers choose to enjoy the festival–downtown or at *Parc Hardy*–they'll be able to view the parade.

Crawfish were an important part of the lives of Cajuns living in Breaux Bridge long before the start of the Crawfish Festival. Using their Gallic culinary skills and cooking secrets handed down from mother to daughter, father to son, the Cajuns transformed the crawfish into a culinary delicacy.

Today housewives make extra money peeling crawfish during the crawfish season at local packing plants. Other residents supplement their income by fishing for crawfish in the nearby Atchafalaya Swamp. For others crawfish farming has become an occupation.

Crawfish Boulettes

- 1 1/2 tablespoons butter, melted
- 1/2 cup chopped onion
- 1/2 cup chopped celery
- 1/4 cup chopped green bell pepper
- 1 pound ground crawfish tails
- 2 tablespoons chopped parsley
- 1/4 cup chopped green onion
- 3 eggs, beaten
- 1 cup Italian seasoned breadcrumbs
- 1/2 teaspoon salt
- 1/2 teaspoon cayenne pepper

1. Preheat oven to 350 degrees F.
2. Melt butter in a heavy skillet.
3. Add onion, celery, and green bell pepper. Sauté until limp.
4. Remove from heat.
5. In a 2-quart bowl, mix ground crawfish, chopped parsley, green onion, beaten eggs, breadcrumbs, and seasonings.
6. Stir sautéed vegetables into crawfish mixture.
7. Mix well.
8. Shape mixture into 24 bite-size, oblong boulettes.
9. Place boulettes on baking sheet.
10. Bake for 20 to 25 minutes.
11. Set aside until ready to add to Bisque. (Recipe follows.)

Yield: 24 boulettes

Each boulette contains:

Calories	117	Protein	2.2 g
Carbohydrate	17.3 g	Sodium	228 mg
Total Fat	4.6 g	Cholesterol	36 mg
		Saturated Fat	3.3 g

St. Martin Parish Homemakers

Crawfish Bisque

1 recipe of Crawfish Boulettes (recipe on facing page)

1/2 cup Lou Ana Vegetable Oil

7 tablespoons all-purpose flour

1/4 cup chopped green bell pepper

1 cup chopped onion

1/2 cup chopped celery

1/2 pound crawfish tails

1 quart water

1 teaspoon salt

1/2 teaspoon black pepper

1/4 teaspoon red pepper

1/2 cup chopped green onion

3 sprigs parsley, chopped

❶ Prepare Boulettes as directed. (See Crawfish Boulettes recipe.)

❷ Place Lou Ana Vegetable Oil in a heavy saucepan. Add flour. Brown until copper colored; stir constantly.

❸ Add green bell pepper, onion, celery. Sauté until limp.

❹ Add crawfish tails, boiling water, and seasonings.

❺ Cook mixture about 15 minutes.

❻ Add boulettes and simmer 30 minutes.

❼ Add green onion and parsley. Simmer 30 minutes.

❽ Serve over cooked rice.

Yield: 7 cups (without rice)
Makes 8 servings

Each serving contains:
Calories 637
Carbohydrate .... 81 g
Total Fat ....32.3 g
Protein .... 9.2 g
Sodium .... 1062 mg
Cholesterol .... 108 mg
Saturated Fat ..... 17.5 g

St. Martin Parish Homemakers

Crawfish Stuffed Peppers

3 tablespoons butter

3/4 cup chopped onion

1/2 cup chopped celery

1 pound crawfish tails

1 teaspoon salt

1/2 teaspoon cayenne pepper

1 cup Italian seasoned breadcrumbs

2 tablespoons chopped green onion

2 tablespoons chopped parsley

1 cup water, divided

2 large green bell peppers

1. Preheat oven to 350 degrees F.
2. In a heavy skillet or saucepan, melt butter over medium heat.
3. Add onion and celery. Cook, stirring constantly until vegetables are limp.
4. Add crawfish tails, salt and cayenne pepper. Sauté until crawfish tails are cooked throughout (about 10 minutes).
5. Remove from heat and add the breadcrumbs, green onion and parsley, and mix thoroughly.
6. Stir in 1/4 cup of water.
7. Cut the green bell peppers lengthwise into thirds and stuff each piece with the filling; pack well.
8. Place stuffed peppers skin side down in 9" x 13" x 2" baking pan.
9. Pour 3/4 cup of hot water into bottom of pan.
10. Bake for 20 minutes.
11. Place the peppers under the broiler to finish browning the tops of the peppers.

Yield: 6 stuffed wedges
Makes 3 servings of 2 wedges each

Each serving contains:
Calories 390
Carbohydrate ...... 35.1 g
Total Fat .... 14 g
Protein .... 30.8 g
Sodium .... 1973 mg
Cholesterol .... 140 mg
Saturated Fat .... 7.6 g

St. Martin Parish Homemakers

Crawfish Jambalaya

1. In a 2-quart saucepan, melt butter.
2. Add 1 cup of rice and stir until rice becomes golden brown.
3. Add onion and green bell pepper to rice and sauté until vegetables become limp.
4. Add crawfish tails, salt, and pepper. Cook for 2 to 5 minutes on medium heat.
5. Add boiling water, green onion, parsley and Worcestershire sauce.
6. Bring to a rolling boil.
7. Reduce heat; cover and simmer over low heat for 20 minutes, or until rice is tender.
8. Remove from heat, let stand 5 minutes before serving.

Yield: 6 1/2 cups
Makes 6 servings

Each serving contains:

Calories	324	Protein	15 g
Carbohydrate	29.1 g	Sodium	653 mg
Total Fat	16.2 g	Cholesterol	97 mg
		Saturated Fat	9.7 g

St. Martin Parish Homemakers

1/2 cup butter

1 cup long- or medium-grain rice, uncooked

1 cup chopped onion

1/2 cup chopped green bell pepper

1 pound crawfish tails

1 teaspoon salt

1 teaspoon cayenne pepper

2 cups boiling water

1/2 cup chopped green onion tops

1/4 cup chopped parsley

1 teaspoon Worcestershire sauce

Crawfish Pie

- 1 pre-baked pie shell (9-inch)
- 1/2 cup butter
- 1/3 cup all-purpose flour
- 1 large garlic clove, chopped
- 1 cup chopped onion
- 5/8 cup chopped green onion bottoms
- 1/2 cup chopped green bell pepper
- 1/2 cup chopped celery
- 4 1/2 teaspoons tomato sauce
- 1 1/2 cups warm water
- 1 1/2 pounds crawfish tails
- 3/4 cup green onion tops
- 3/8 cup chopped parsley
- 1/2 teaspoon salt
- 1/2 teaspoon cayenne pepper
- 1/2 teaspoon black pepper
- 2 tablespoons all-purpose flour
- 2 tablespoons water

1. Preheat oven to 425 degrees F.
2. Bake 9" pie shell. Set aside. (Note: Check after 8 minutes.)
3. In heavy saucepan, melt butter.
4. Add flour and brown lightly.
5. Add garlic, onion, green onion bottoms, green bell pepper, celery and tomato sauce.
6. Cover and place on a low heat setting. Cook until vegetables are tender. Stir frequently to keep from sticking.
7. Add 1 1/2 cups of warm water and simmer for 1 hour, stirring to prevent sticking. Mixture should be creamy and thick.
8. Add crawfish tails, green onion tops, parsley, and seasonings.
9. Blend 2 tablespoons of flour with 2 tablespoons of water. Add to the crawfish mixture, stirring until mixture thickens over medium heat (about 2 minutes).
10. Pour into baked pie shell.
11. Serve immediately.

Yield: 1 pie (9-inch)
Makes 8 servings

Each serving contains:

Calories	652	Protein	6.8 g
Carbohydrate	83.4 g	Sodium	821 mg
Total Fat	34.4 g	Cholesterol	31 mg
		Saturated Fat	20.9 g

St. Martin Parish Homemakers

Filé Crawfish Gumbo

1/2 cup Lou Ana Vegetable Oil

1 cup all-purpose flour

1 onion, chopped

8 cups hot water

3 pods garlic, minced

1 pound crawfish tails

1/4 cup chopped parsley

1/4 cup chopped onion tops

1/4 cup chopped celery leaves

2 teaspoons salt

1/2 teaspoon red pepper

1/2 teaspoon black pepper

1. Make a roux by cooking Lou Ana Vegetable Oil and flour together to a golden brown color, stirring constantly.
2. Add onion and cook until wilted.
3. Add hot water.
4. Simmer on low heat for 30 minutes.
5. Add garlic and crawfish tails; let simmer for 25 minutes.
6. Add parsley, green onion tops, and celery leaves and simmer 5 minutes.
7. Season with salt, red pepper and black pepper.
8. Serve in soup plates with hot steamed rice, and Tabasco sauce, if desired.

Yield: 10 cups (without rice)
Makes 10 servings

Each serving contains:

Calories	196	Protein	9.2 g
Carbohydrate	13.4 g	Sodium	525 mg
Total Fat	11.5 g	Cholesterol	32 mg
		Saturated Fat	2.8 g

St. Martin Parish Homemakers

Crawfish Etouffee

1/2 cup butter

1/3 cup chopped onion

1/8 cup chopped green onion

1/4 cup chopped green bell pepper

1 pound peeled crawfish

1/8 teaspoon Accent

1 teaspoon paprika

1/8 teaspoon red pepper

1/4 teaspoon black pepper

1/4 teaspoon salt

5/8 cup water, divided

1/4 cup cornstarch

1/8 cup chopped green onion tops

1. In a heavy skillet containing melted butter, sauté onion, green onion, and bell pepper.
2. Add crawfish, Accent, seasonings and 1/2 cup of water. Cook for five minutes.
3. In a small bowl mix cornstarch with 1/8 cup of water.
4. Add cornstarch paste to crawfish mixture, stirring constantly.
5. Add green onion tops. Cook for 5 to 10 minutes, stirring as needed.
6. Serve over cooked rice.

Yield: 2 1/2 cups (without rice)
Makes 5 servings (1/2 cup each)

Each serving contains:
Calories 252
Carbohydrate .... 5.6 g
Total Fat .... 18.9 g
Protein .... 15.2 g
Sodium .... 422 mg
Cholesterol .... 115 mg
Saturated Fat ..... 11.5 g

Michael A. Wiltz

Crawfish Fettuccine

1. Cook fettuccine noodles as directed on package. (Use 3 quarts of water and 1 tablespoon of salt.) Drain.
2. In a heavy 2-quart saucepan, melt butter.
3. Add onion, green onion, and green bell pepper. Sauté until limp.
4. Add crawfish and cook five minutes.
5. Add flour; mix well.
6. Add milk and chicken-flavored base. Continue cooking, stirring constantly until mixture thickens.
7. Add wine and seasonings. Stir to mix.
8. Add sauce to cooked, drained noodles. Stir until noodles and sauce are well-mixed.

Yield: 9 cups
Makes 9 servings

Each serving contains:

Calories	291	Protein	13.9 g
Carbohydrate	28.1 g	Sodium	373 mg
Total Fat	13.3 g	Cholesterol	96 mg
		Saturated Fat	7.2 g

Michael A. Wiltz
Overall Winner, 1987

1 pound fettuccine noodles

3 quarts water

1 tablespoon salt

1/2 cup butter

1/2 cup chopped onion

1/8 cup chopped green onion

1/4 cup chopped green bell pepper

1 pound peeled crawfish

1/2 cup all-purpose flour

1 1/2 cups milk

3 tablespoons chicken-flavored base

1/2 ounce white wine

1/4 teaspoon red pepper

1/2 teaspoon black pepper

Tony O. CHAMPAGNE

Cattle Festival Steers Tourists to Abbeville

Abbeville

It's no bull that the Cattle Festival, held annually on the first weekend in October in Abbeville, is a roundup of fun that celebrates this important Louisiana-wide industry.

The festival began in 1949 as the Dairy Festival, but the event was branded with a new name in 1979 to honor all phases of the cattle industry.

Total income to Louisiana from the beef industry in 1989 was over $265 million, and Abbeville area farms contributed significantly to this sum.

An average of 30,000 persons–more than twice the population of Abbeville–stampede into town for the weekend-long event. Highlights of the festival include the crowning of a festival queen and junior queen, a parade and a street dance held in quaint downtown Abbeville on opening night.

There's plenty of festival food to enjoy, arts and crafts booths, live entertainment, a livestock show and, of course, a rodeo.

The festival was begun under the auspices of the Abbeville Chamber of Commerce and its manager at the time, Roy Theriot. Today a portion of the proceeds from the festival are used to sponsor 4-H events for area students.

Creole Steak

- 2 tablespoons all-purpose flour
- 1 teaspoon Creole seasoning
- 1 teaspoon paprika
- 1/2 teaspoon red pepper
- 4 eye of round steaks, 1/2 inch thick (one pound)
- 1 cup chopped onion
- 1/2 cup chopped green bell pepper
- 3 teaspoons butter, divided
- 1/2 cup uncooked rice
- 1 teaspoon salt
- 1/4 teaspoon red pepper
- 16 ounces stewed tomatoes
- 1 cup water

1. Preheat oven to 350 degrees F.
2. Combine flour, Creole seasoning, paprika, and red pepper.
3. Pound each steak with a meat mallet.
4. Dredge steak in flour mixture.
5. In oven-proof skillet, cook onion and green bell pepper in one teaspoon of butter until tender; remove from skillet.
6. Brown meat in remaining two teaspoons of butter in same skillet; cover meat with onion mixture; sprinkle with rice.
7. Add salt and red pepper.
8. Spoon tomatoes over rice; mix remaining flour mixture with water. Blend well.
9. Pour water-flour mixture over meat mixture.
10. Cover and bake for 1 hour.
11. Let stand 15 minutes.
12. Spoon into serving platter. Garnish as desired.

Serves 4

Each serving contains:
Calories 322
Carbohydrate ...... 30.8 g
Total Fat .... 9.1 g
Protein .... 28.7 g
Sodium .... 1114 mg
Cholesterol .... 74 mg
Saturated Fat .... 3.9 g

Mrs. Irene B. Prejean
Second Place, Adult Division, Main Dish

Slenderella Beef

- 4 (4-ounce size) eye of round steaks
- 1 teaspoon salt
- 1/4 teaspoon white pepper
- 3 tablespoons dry white wine
- 2 teaspoons prepared mustard
- 2 tablespoons butter
- Water, as needed
- 2 tablespoons minced onion
- 1 tablespoon minced fresh parsley
- 1 clove garlic, minced
- 1/2 teaspoon ground thyme
- 1 teaspoon pimientos

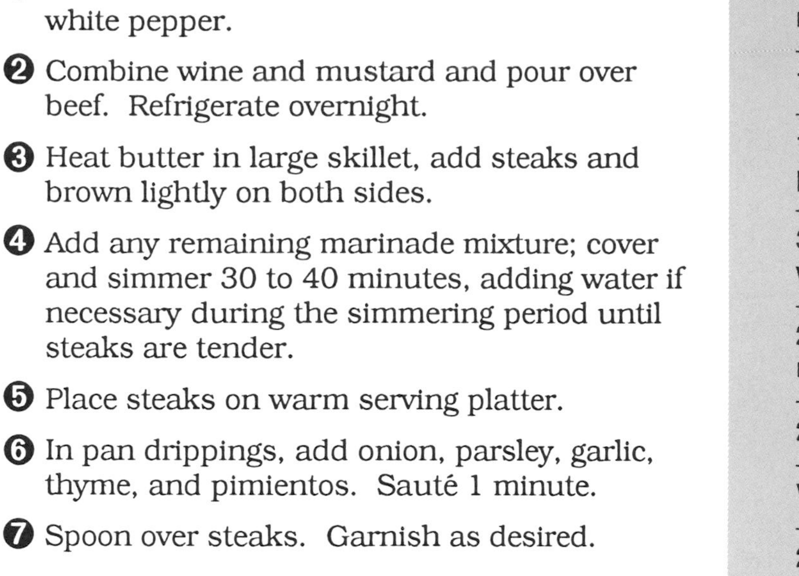

1. Pound steaks and trim. Season with salt and white pepper.
2. Combine wine and mustard and pour over beef. Refrigerate overnight.
3. Heat butter in large skillet, add steaks and brown lightly on both sides.
4. Add any remaining marinade mixture; cover and simmer 30 to 40 minutes, adding water if necessary during the simmering period until steaks are tender.
5. Place steaks on warm serving platter.
6. In pan drippings, add onion, parsley, garlic, thyme, and pimientos. Sauté 1 minute.
7. Spoon over steaks. Garnish as desired.

Serves 4 (1 steak per serving)

Each serving contains:

Calories	222	Protein	25.3 g
Carbohydrate	1.2 g	Sodium	736 mg
Total Fat	11.4 g	Cholesterol	82 mg
		Saturated Fat	5.5 g

Mrs. Amson "Delta" Corner
First Place, Low-Calorie Main Dishes, Adult Division

Mini Beef Sandwich

- 1 pound ground chuck
- 1/2 cup chopped onion
- 1/4 cup chopped green bell pepper
- 1/4 cup chopped celery
- 1/2 cup shredded Monterey Jack cheese with jalapeno peppers
- 1/4 cup sandwich spread
- 1/2 teaspoon salt
- 18 slices day-old bread, crust removed
- 1/4 cup butter, softened
- 4 eggs
- 1/2 cup water
- 1/4 cup Lou Ana Vegetable Oil for grilling
- Grated Parmesan cheese

1. Stir-fry beef, onion, bell pepper and celery until meat is no longer pink.
2. Drain excess fat.
3. Stir in shredded cheese, sandwich spread, and salt. Mix well.
4. Butter one side of each slice of bread.
5. Spread meat mixture equally on nine of the bread slices.
6. Put sandwich together.
7. Cut each sandwich into two triangles.
8. Beat eggs and water together.
9. Dip sandwiches one at a time in egg mixture and grill on hot griddle lightly greased with Lou Ana Vegetable Oil. Grill until golden brown on both sides.
10. Sprinkle with Parmesan cheese, if desired.

Yield: 18 mini-sandwiches

1 mini-sandwich has:

Calories	185	Protein	8.1 g
Carbohydrate	8 g	Sodium	255 mg
Total Fat	13.3 g	Cholesterol	91 mg
		Saturated Fat	5.2 g

Mr. Amson Corner
Grand Champion Winner, Adult Division, 1987

Beef-Stuffed Peppers

- 5 green bell peppers
- 1 pound ground chuck
- 1 1/2 cups chopped onion
- 8 ounces tomato sauce
- 8 3/4 ounces drained whole-kernel corn
- 2 teaspoons chili powder
- 1/2 teaspoon salt
- 1/2 cup shredded cheddar cheese

1. Preheat oven to 350 degrees F.
2. Cut tops from green bell peppers, remove centers and discard.
3. Cook peppers 5 minutes in boiling water, drain peppers and set aside.
4. Cook ground beef and onion in a large skillet until meat is browned, stirring to crumble meat; drain well.
5. Stir in tomato sauce, corn, chili powder, and salt.
6. Stuff peppers with meat mixture and place in a baking dish.
7. Bake for 15 minutes.
8. Sprinkle tops of peppers with cheese. Bake an additional 5 minutes.

Yield: 5 stuffed peppers
Makes 5 servings

Each pepper contains:
Calories 286
Carbohydrate ...... 26.9 g
Total Fat .... 9.6 g
Protein .... 26.2 g
Sodium .... 385 mg
Cholesterol .... 66 mg
Saturated Fat .... 4.3 g

Rosalyn Abshire

Loose Cabbage Rolls

1 1/2 pounds ground chuck

1 1/2 cups chopped onion

1/2 cup chopped green bell pepper

2 stalks celery, chopped

1/2 cup uncooked rice

1 teaspoon salt

1 1/2 teaspoons black pepper

1 head cabbage, coarsely shredded*

12 ounces V-8 juice

1. Preheat oven to 350 degrees F.
2. Sauté ground chuck, onion, green bell pepper, and celery.
3. Remove from heat; add rice, salt, and black pepper.
4. Layer cabbage and meat mixture in a 2-quart casserole dish.
5. Pour V-8 juice over top of mixture.
6. Cover and cook for 1 1/2 hours.

*Use 2 to 2 1/2 pounds of cabbage.

Yield: Approximately 11 cups
Makes 11 servings (1 cup each)

Each serving contains:

Calories	150	Protein	15.2 g
Carbohydrate	14.7 g	Sodium	391 mg
Total Fat	3.5 g	Cholesterol	37 mg
		Saturated Fat	1.2 g

Jenny Trahan
Beef Main Dish, Junior Division

Simply Elegant Steak & Rice

1. Cut steak into thin strips.
2. Brown meat in Lou Ana Vegetable Oil, using high heat.
3. Add onions and sauté.
4. Blend soup, liquid from mushrooms, black pepper, and seasoned salt. Pour over steak.
5. Add mushrooms.
6. Add water, reduce heat, cover and simmer for one hour.
7. Serve over beds of fluffy rice.

Yield: 4 3/4 cups of steak entree plus 3 cups of rice
Makes 6 servings

Each serving contains:

Calories	365	Protein	28.1 g
Carbohydrate	33.9 g	Sodium	1001 mg
Total Fat	11.6 g	Cholesterol	70 mg
		Saturated Fat	3.2 g

Jill Broussard
Grand Champion Winner, Junior Division, 1987

1 1/2 pounds boneless beef round steak

1 1/2 tablespoons Lou Ana Vegetable Oil

2 large onions, cut into 1/2-inch slices (Separate into rings.)

1 can (10 3/4 ounces) cream of mushroom soup

1 can (4 ounces) sliced mushrooms

1/2 teaspoon black pepper

1/2 teaspoon seasoned salt

1 cup water

3 cups hot cooked rice

Macedonian Beef Stew

- 1 pound beef stew meat
- 1/2 teaspoon salt
- 1/4 teaspoon white pepper
- 1 tablespoon all-purpose flour
- 6 tablespoons Lou Ana Vegetable Oil
- 2 cups chopped onion
- 3 garlic cloves, minced
- 2 cups thinly sliced cabbage
- 1/4 teaspoon crushed marjoram leaves
- 1/4 teaspoon crumbled rosemary
- 1/4 teaspoon crushed sweet basil leaves
- 1/4 teaspoon crushed thyme leaves
- 1/2 cup water
- 1 can (14 1/2 ounces) Cajun stewed tomatoes
- 1 can (10 1/2 ounces) beef broth
- 1 can (16 ounces) plain navy beans
- 2 tablespoons chopped parsley

1. Slice beef thinly across grain. Season with salt and white pepper.
2. Dust with flour.
3. Heat Lou Ana Vegetable Oil in Dutch oven.
4. Stir-fry beef until lightly browned.
5. Transfer with slotted spoon to bowl.
6. Stir-fry onion, garlic, and cabbage in pan drippings until golden.
7. Add marjoram, rosemary, basil, and thyme.
8. Add water, tomatoes, and broth; bring to a boil.
9. Add beef, cover and simmer 30 to 35 minutes.
10. Add beans, cover, and simmer another 15 minutes.
11. Sprinkle with chopped parsley for garnish.

Yield: 7 cups
Makes 7 servings

Each serving contains:

Calories	311
Carbohydrate	21.7 g
Total Fat	15.5 g
Protein	21.2 g
Sodium	730 mg
Cholesterol	37 mg
Saturated Fat	4.2 g

Mrs. Amson "Delta" Corner
First Place, Beef Main Dishes, Adult Division

Deviled Swiss Steak

- 2 1/2 pounds round steak, cut one-inch thick
- 1/2 teaspoon salt
- 1/4 teaspoon black pepper
- 1/4 cup all-purpose flour
- 3 tablespoons Lou Ana Vegetable Oil
- 1 cup chopped onion
- 3 cups whole canned tomatoes
- 1 can (8 ounces) tomato sauce
- 1 garlic clove, chopped fine
- 1/2 can (10 3/4-ounce size) cream of mushroom soup
- 1 1/2 teaspoons Worcestershire sauce
- 1/2 cup chopped green bell pepper

1. Season meat with salt and black pepper. Pound flour into meat.
2. In large skillet, brown meat on both sides in hot Lou Ana Vegetable Oil.
3. Top with onion, tomatoes, tomato sauce, garlic, soup, and Worcestershire sauce.
4. Cover; cook on low heat until tender (about 2 hours).
5. Add green bell pepper about half an hour before dish is done.
6. Remove from heat. Serve immediately.

Serves 8

Each serving contains:

Calories	338	Protein	34.3 g
Carbohydrate	18.7 g	Sodium	657 mg
Total Fat	13.7 g	Cholesterol	82 mg
		Saturated Fat	3.9 g

Becky Broussard
Fourth Place, Main Dishes, Adult Division

Beef Sauce Piquante

1 pound eye of round steak

1 teaspoon Creole seasoning

2 tablespoons Lou Ana Vegetable Oil, divided

1 1/2 tablespoons all-purpose flour

1/2 cup chopped onion

1/4 cup chopped green bell pepper

1/4 cup chopped celery

1/4 cup chopped canned mushrooms

1/4 cup Ro-Tel tomatoes with chilies

3/4 cup water

1/2 cup chopped green onion

1/2 cup chopped parsley

1. Cut steak into bite-size pieces.
2. Sprinkle with Creole seasoning; mix and set aside for 15 minutes.
3. Brown meat in medium saucepan in 1 tablespoon Lou Ana Vegetable Oil; set aside.
4. In medium saucepan, make roux with flour and remaining 1 tablespoon Lou Ana Vegetable Oil.
5. Add onion, green bell pepper, celery, mushrooms, and meat; cook 5 minutes.
6. Add Ro-Tel tomatoes and water. Cook 15 minutes.
7. Add green onion and parsley. Cook covered 45 minutes or until desired tenderness. If necessary, additional water may be added.
8. Pour into serving dish. Garnish if desired.

Makes 4 servings (approximately 1 cup each)

Each serving contains:

Calories	250	Protein	26.3 g
Carbohydrate	6.7 g	Sodium	369 mg
Total Fat	12.5 g	Cholesterol	67 mg
		Saturated Fat	3.7 g

Mrs. Irene B. Prejean
Second Place, Adult Division, Main Dishes

Chili

1. Season meat with black pepper and Creole seasoning.
2. Brown meat and drain fat.
3. Add green bell pepper, celery, jalapeno pepper, and onion. Cook until soft.
4. Add tomato sauce, chili powder, oregano, and flour. Mix well. Cook for 5 minutes over medium heat.
5. Add water to cover meat.
6. Add beans. Simmer for 45 minutes to an hour, stirring occasionally.

Yield: approximately 7 cups
Makes 7 servings (1 cup each)

Each serving contains:

Calories	158	Protein	17.1 g
Carbohydrate	14.1 g	Sodium	361 mg
Total Fat	4.2 g	Cholesterol	40 mg
		Saturated Fat	1.5 g

April Petry
Fifth Place, Main Dish Category

1/2 teaspoon black pepper

1/2 teaspoon Creole seasoning

1 pound ground chuck

1 green bell pepper, chopped

2 stalks celery, chopped

1 tablespoon chopped jalapeno pepper

1 1/2 cups chopped onion

15 ounces tomato sauce

2 tablespoons chili powder

1/2 teaspoon oregano

2 tablespoons all-purpose flour

4 cups water

1 can (15 ounces) red kidney beans

TONY O. CHAMPAGNE

A Gigantic Celebration of Acadian Life

Lafayette

Festivals Acadiens in Lafayette is an annual fall celebration of all forms of Cajun life–past, present and future.

Crowds of more than 150,000 visit this festival, which is actually several festivals rolled into one September weekend. The crowds are accommodated with a variety of festival sites and free parking at the Cajundome with bus service to the sites.

One aspect of the festival is the Louisiana Native Crafts Festival, which includes demonstrations by native artisans, a segment entitled "How Men Cook," music by Cajun artists, and story-telling. Strolling the grounds of the Lafayette Natural History Museum, festival visitors will also see Indian tool-making, sheep-shearing, indigo-dyeing and saddle-making.

The *Festival de Musique Acadienne* is held under the oak trees of nearby Girard Park. This event is sponsored by the Lafayette Jaycees and provides plenty of two-stepping music for festival-goers.

Authentic Cajun cuisine is featured at the Bayou Food Festival, where area restaurateurs and chefs provide cooking demonstrations and offer samples of seafood gumbo, crawfish etouffee, stuffed flounder and more.

Favorite regional foods and exotic new creations can be sampled at the glamorous Culinary Classic, an official competition of the American Culinary Federation, in which area member chefs compete for gold, silver and bronze medals.

The Acadiana Fair and Trade Show, a carnival, a Kids Alive! program in downtown Lafayette, and a Senior Fair and Craft Show round out the fun at this festival geared for all ages.

Tomato & Crab Bisque

8 cups water or seafood stock

1 cup blonde roux (browned flour)

1 1/2 cups tomato paste

1/2 teaspoon cayenne pepper

1 tablespoon onion powder

1 tablespoon garlic powder

2 teaspoons salt

1 tablespoon fresh chopped basil

1 teaspoon fresh lemon thyme

1 tablespoon fresh chopped green onion

1 tablespoon fresh parsley

1/2 pound lump crabmeat

1. Bring water or stock to a boil over medium heat.
2. Mix in roux and tomato paste. Blend thoroughly.
3. Add remaining ingredients, except crabmeat.
4. Lower heat and simmer for 10 minutes, stirring frequently.
5. Add crabmeat about 3 minutes before serving.

Yield: 9 cups
Makes 9 servings

Each serving contains:

Calories	166	Protein	7.2 g
Carbohydrate	15.9 g	Sodium	805 mg
Total Fat	8.7 g	Cholesterol	25 mg
		Saturated Fat	2 g

Chris Sogga
Line Cook, Hotel Acadiana, Lafayette, La.
Gold Medal Winner, Soup Category
Culinary Classic Competition

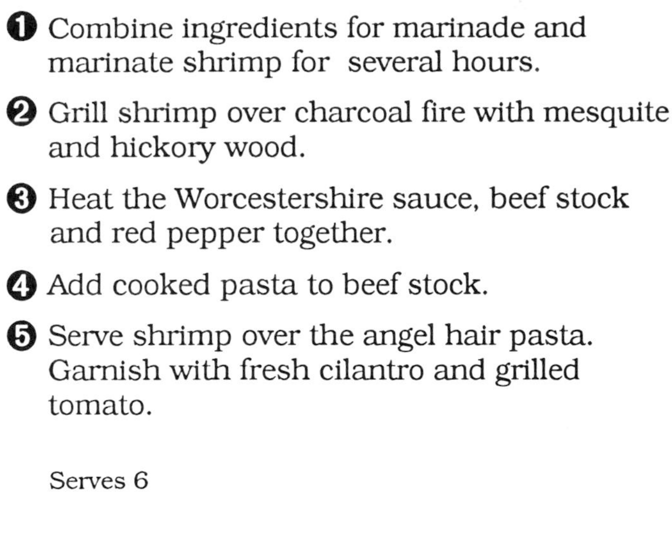

Kahlua Grilled Shrimp On Angel Hair Pasta

1. Combine ingredients for marinade and marinate shrimp for several hours.
2. Grill shrimp over charcoal fire with mesquite and hickory wood.
3. Heat the Worcestershire sauce, beef stock and red pepper together.
4. Add cooked pasta to beef stock.
5. Serve shrimp over the angel hair pasta. Garnish with fresh cilantro and grilled tomato.

Serves 6

Each serving contains:

Calories	572	Protein	47.3 g
Carbohydrate	60.9 g	Sodium	1255 mg
Total Fat	15.2 g	Cholesterol	336 mg
		Saturated Fat	1.6 g

Ken Veron
Chef-Owner, Cafe Vermilionville
Gold Medal Winner in the Seafood Category
1988 Acadiana Culinary Classic

2 pounds peeled shrimp (21-25 count)

MARINADE

1 cup Kahlua

1 1/2 cups honey

1 1/2 cups Lou Ana Peanut Oil

2 bottles Tiger Sauce (10-ounce size)

2 tablespoons seasoned salt

2 tablespoons chopped garlic

2 tablespoons chopped parsley

2 ounces hot pepper sauce

2 tablespoons chopped basil

2 tablespoons chopped thyme

2 tablespoons chopped cilantro

♦

2 tablespoons Worcestershire sauce

4 cups beef stock

3 tablespoons chopped red pepper

1 pound angel hair pasta

Baked Vegetables In Sour Cream

- 2 cups chopped green bell pepper
- 2/3 cup chopped green onion
- 3 tablespoons butter
- 1 1/2 cups grated carrots
- 1/2 cup minced parsley
- 4 yellow squash, cut into 1/2" x 2" strips
- 1/2 teaspoon basil
- 1/2 teaspoon oregano
- 1/2 teaspoon white pepper
- 1 cup sour cream
- 2/3 cup freshly grated Romano
- 1/2 cup freshly grated Romano

1. Preheat oven to 350 degrees F.
2. In a large skillet, sauté the green bell pepper and green onion in butter for 3 minutes.
3. Add carrots and parsley and sauté for another three minutes.
4. Add yellow squash and cook three more minutes and then add the basil, oregano, and white pepper.
5. Remove skillet from heat; add the sour cream and 2/3 cup of Romano and combine the mixture well.
6. Pour into a buttered 1 1/2-quart soufflé dish.
7. Sprinkle the top with 1/2 cup of Romano.
8. Bake for 35 minutes.

Yield: 4 cups
Makes 4 servings

Each serving contains:

Calories	375	Protein	13.5 g
Carbohydrate	16.9 g	Sodium	491 mg
Total Fat	29.3 g	Cholesterol	79 mg
		Saturated Fat	18.1 g

Chef Anna D. Thoman
Elton, La.
Culinary Classic Competition

Veal Supreme

1 1/2-pound saddle of veal or fillet of veal, cut into 2 1/2-inch squares

6 tablespoons unsalted butter or Lou Ana Pan and Grill frying oil

1 cup Curry Sauce (Recipe follows)

1 whole pineapple, peeled, cored and sliced into thin strips

3 cups sliced or split almonds, lightly toasted

1 teaspoon salt

1/8 teaspoon ground black pepper

1 cup hollandaise sauce

❶ Cook veal in butter approximately 1 minute on each side.

❷ Remove from pan.

❸ Pour off fat and add Curry Sauce.

❹ Bring to a boil and boil for 3 minutes.

❺ Add veal and pineapple.

❻ Bring back to a boil. Add 2 cups of almonds, salt, and pepper.

❼ Remove pan from heat and stir in hollandaise sauce. (Do not let it boil or it will curdle.)

❽ Slide contents of pan onto a plate of silver or a metal dish.

❾ Garnish with remaining cup of almonds.

♦

CURRY SAUCE

2 apples, peeled and finely chopped

1 mashed banana

1 fresh pineapple, peeled and cut into small cubes

3 tablespoons butter

1/4 cup all-purpose flour

1/4 cup curry powder

2 tablespoons shredded coconut

4 1/2 cups chicken stock

Combine all ingredients of Curry Sauce and simmer one hour. This will yield 7 1/2 cups of Curry Sauce. Only one cup is used in the recipe. The rest may be saved for later use.

Makes 6 servings

Each serving contains:
Calories 892
Carbohydrate ...... 32.4 g
Total Fat .... 72.3 g
Protein .... 37.1 g
Sodium .... 779 mg
Cholesterol .... 224 mg
Saturated Fat ..... 23.4 g

Chef Bill O'Dea
Executive Chef, Hotel Acadiana, Lafayette, La.
Gold Medal Winner, Culinary Classic Competition

Fried Eggplant Rounds With Chicken Cream Sauce

1 tablespoon butter

1/2 pound chicken breast, cut into 1" strips

1/4 cup thinly sliced mushrooms

1/4 teaspoon red pepper

1/4 teaspoon white pepper

1/4 teaspoon salt

1 cup Half & Half cream

1/2 cup finely chopped green onion

CREAM SAUCE

1. Melt butter in a heavy skillet over medium heat.
2. Add the chicken, mushrooms, red pepper, white pepper and salt.
3. Cook 5 minutes, stirring often. Stir in the cream and cook about 5 minutes longer.
4. Add green onion and cook an additional 2 minutes or until sauce thickens.

FRIED EGGPLANT

- 1/4 teaspoon salt
- 1/4 teaspoon white pepper
- 1/4 teaspoon red pepper
- 1 eggplant, peeled and sliced into 1" rounds
- 1 cup milk
- 1 egg
- 1 cup Lou Ana Vegetable Oil, for frying
- 1 cup all-purpose flour
- 1 cup dry breadcrumbs

1. In a small bowl, combine the salt and pepper; mix well and sprinkle the seasoning over both sides of the eggplant; set aside.
2. In a medium bowl, beat together milk and egg; set aside.
3. Heat oil in a heavy skillet over high heat until very hot.
4. Dredge the eggplant in flour; then dip in egg mixture; then dredge in breadcrumbs.
5. Carefully drop into hot oil and fry 3 minutes or until golden brown; remove and drain on paper towels.
6. Place eggplant on a plate and top with Cream Sauce.

Yield: 4 servings (2 slices per serving)

Each serving contains:

Calories	413	Protein	18.7 g
Carbohydrate	26 g	Sodium	546 mg
Total Fat	26 g	Cholesterol	69 mg
		Saturated Fat	9.1 g

Enola Prudhomme, Chef/Owner
Prudhomme's Cajun Cafe, Carencro, La.
Culinary Classic Compètition

Best Pork Roast

- 1 pork butt (4-5 pounds)
- 1 teaspoon salt, divided
- 1 teaspoon black pepper, divided
- 13 garlic cloves, cut in half (use more if desired)
- 1 tablespoon seasoned salt, divided
- 2 cups chopped onion
- 1 1/2 cups white wine, divided

1. Preheat oven to 350 degrees F.
2. Debone roast. Salt and pepper it. Turn it fat side down.
3. Make incisions in the shape of a cross, about 1/4 inch each way and about 1 1/2 inches apart.
4. Insert 1/2 clove of garlic in each incision. (Do not worry about too much garlic flavor. More is better than not enough.)
5. After garlic is placed in each hole, put seasonings inside.
6. Place chopped onion on bottom of roasting pan.
7. Put roast in the pan, bottom side up (fat down).
8. Pour wine over roast.
9. Sprinkle salt, pepper, and seasoned salt on roast.
10. Turn roast over, fat side up, and insert more garlic in incisions and a mixture of garlic and onion in the place where the bone was taken out in deboning.

⓫ Pour wine in this split; then sprinkle with salt, pepper, and seasoned salt.

⓬ Place flat side down and pour wine on fat; then place chopped onion and garlic on top of roast. (You should have about 3/4 to one inch of wine in the bottom of the pan.)

⓭ Bake roast at 350 degrees F. until it has an internal temperature of 160 degrees F. or until it is tender, about 2 1/2 hours.

⓮ The gravy may be used as it is or thickened with roux or any way you wish.

Makes 16 servings (3 ounces per serving)

Each serving contains:*

Calories	220	Protein	25.5 g
Carbohydrate	0.1 g	Sodium	170 mg
Total Fat	12.3 g	Cholesterol	88 mg
		Saturated Fat	4.3 g

* *Roast only*

Chef Ray Thoman
Elton, La.
Culinary Classic Competition

Tony O.Champagne

On Roasting Pork, Hot Boudin and Sizzling Cracklin

Basile

There's an old saying around Evangeline Parish that the pig is a farmer's best friend because every part of him can be used except the squeal.

Even the squeal gets put to use at the Swine Festival, held the first weekend in November in Basile. A hog-calling contest is a highlight of this festival, which was started in 1966 to promote the thriving swine industry of the area. Today the industry has declined significantly, but the festival continues.

Whiffs of good things to come greet visitors as they arrive at the festival, held at Basile's town park. The pungent aromas of roasting pork, sizzling cracklin, sausage and steaming boudin permeate the cool fall air.

On Saturday, while youngsters busy themselves with carnival rides, pork lovers can begin their feasting. Booths are set up to sell every conceivable pork delicacy known to people in this pork-loving area. Carnival staples such as hot dogs and hamburgers are available, but a favorite booth is the one manned by the Knights of Columbus, where they serve delicious pork roast sandwiches.

A novel event at the Swine Festival is the Dress the Piglet Contest. It's not easy to put clothes on a squealing, wiggling piglet.

Sunday at the festival brings a parade, live Cajun music for street dancing and barbecue pork dinners, again, from the Knights of Columbus. Following the parade there are boudin-eating, hog-calling and greased pig contests.

Live music, the crowning of King Porky and Queen Petunia and a weekend-long arts and crafts show are among the other attractions that bring 14,000 people annually to this festival.

Fried Pork Pies

1 1/2 tablespoons Lou Ana Vegetable Oil

1 tablespoon all-purpose flour

1/4 pound ground chuck

3/4 pound ground pork

1 cup chopped onion

1/2 cup chopped green onion including tops

1/4 cup parsley

1/2 teaspoon salt

1/4 teaspoon black pepper

1/4 teaspoon red pepper

1/2 teaspoon oregano

FILLING

1. Mix Lou Ana Vegetable Oil and flour in a 10-inch skillet.
2. Add next four ingredients.
3. Cook until meat is no longer pink.
4. Add seasonings.
5. Drain excess oil from the mixture.
6. Cool before placing filling in pastry dough.

PASTRY

1. Sift flour, salt, and baking powder into a 1-quart bowl. Mix well.
2. Cut in shortening.
3. Mix milk and beaten eggs and add to flour mixture.
4. Divide dough into 10 portions. Place one portion on a floured board and roll into a circle approximately 7 inches in diameter. Use a lid or saucer to cut into a circle about 6 inches in diameter.
5. Place several tablespoons of the meat mixture on one side of pastry. Fold dough over. Dampen edges with water. Crimp edges together with a fork. (Make other pies in same manner.)
6. Preheat Lou Ana Vegetable Oil to 350 degrees F. in a deep fat electric fryer.
7. Place pies in oil and fry until golden brown. Remove from oil and drain on absorbent paper.

Yield: 10 pies

Each pie contains:

Calories	401	Protein	13.9 g
Carbohydrate	28.6 g	Sodium	401 mg
Total Fat	25.3 g	Cholesterol	85 mg
		Saturated Fat	6 g

Mrs. Mabel LeDoux
Second Place, 1987

2 1/2 cups all-purpose flour

1 teaspoon salt

1/2 teaspoon baking powder

1/4 cup shortening

2 eggs, beaten

1/2 cup milk

Lou Ana Vegetable Oil

Cabbage-Pork Casserole

- 1 cup water
- 1/2 cup raw rice
- 1/2 small head of cabbage, shredded and cooked only until tender-crisp
- 1 pound regular ground sausage
- 2 tablespoons Lou Ana Vegetable Oil
- 1/4 cup chopped onion
- 1/4 cup chopped green bell pepper
- 1/4 cup chopped celery
- 1/4 teaspoon black pepper
- 1/2 teaspoon salt
- 1 can (8 ounces) tomato sauce
- 3/4 cup shredded American cheese
- 1/4 cup fried bacon, crumbled

1. Preheat oven to 350 degrees F. Grease 2-quart casserole dish.
2. Bring water to a boil in a 1-quart saucepan. Add rice. Return to a boil. Reduce to a simmer. Cover saucepan and cook until rice is tender (20 - 25 minutes).
3. Cook cabbage.
4. Cook sausage.
5. In a small skillet, heat 2 tablespoons of Lou Ana Vegetable Oil. Add onion, green bell pepper, and celery. Sauté until wilted.
6. Add seasonings and onion mixture to the cabbage. Stir together.
7. Layer steamed cabbage, cooked rice, and cooked ground sausage in casserole dish. Repeat to produce 2 layers of each.
8. Pour tomato sauce over all.
9. Bake 20 minutes.
10. Remove from oven.
11. Sprinkle shredded cheese and bacon on top.

Yield: 7 cups
Makes 7 servings (1 cup each)

Each serving contains:

Calories	346	Protein	15.4 g
Carbohydrate	15.4 g	Sodium	1075 mg
Total Fat	24.9 g	Cholesterol	56 mg
		Saturated Fat	9.3 g

Mrs. Charles Bollich
Grand Champion, 1987

Ragout a la Francaise

1. Preheat oven to 350 degrees F.
2. Brown pork chops in Lou Ana Vegetable Oil in skillet.
3. Remove from skillet and place in 1-quart baking dish that has a cover.
4. Sauté green onions in skillet.
5. Mix flour and water. Add to sautéed green onions. Cook until slightly thick.
6. Add salt, pepper, thyme, parsley, and bay leaves. Pour over pork chops.
7. Add potatoes.
8. Cover and bake 1 hour, until pork chops and potatoes are tender.

Makes 2 servings

Each serving contains:

Calories	547	Protein	41.9 g
Carbohydrate	38.4 g	Sodium	1292 mg
Total Fat	24.4 g	Cholesterol	140 mg
		Saturated Fat	8.1 g

Monsieur and Madame Richard Tilly of France
Second Place, 1987

2 pork chops

1 1/2 teaspoons Lou Ana Vegetable Oil

4 green onions, chopped

2 tablespoons all-purpose flour

1 3/4 cups water

1 teaspoon salt

1 teaspoon black pepper

1/2 teaspoon thyme

1 tablespoon parsley

3 bay leaves

2 medium-size white potatoes, quartered

Jambalaya

- 1 pound sausage
- 2 tablespoons Lou Ana Vegetable Oil
- 2 medium onions, chopped
- 1 cup chopped green onion
- 1 green bell pepper, chopped
- 2 garlic cloves, minced
- 1 teaspoon salt
- 1/4 teaspoon black pepper
- 1/8 teaspoon red pepper
- 1 cup raw rice
- 3 cups water

1. Brown sausage in Lou Ana Vegetable Oil heated in heavy skillet. Drain fat that accumulates.
2. When browned, add onion, green onion, green bell pepper, and garlic.
3. Cook over medium heat for 10 minutes. Stir occasionally.
4. Season with salt, black pepper, and red pepper.
5. Place rice with water in large thick pot. Bring to a boil.
6. Add meat mixture to rice and continue to cook and stir over medium heat for 25 to 30 minutes or until rice is tender.

Yield: 8 cups
Makes 8 servings

Each serving contains:

Calories	267	Protein	10.1 g
Carbohydrate	24.9 g	Sodium	791 mg
Total Fat	13.9 g	Cholesterol	31 mg
		Saturated Fat	4.7 g

Mrs. Martha Hester
First Place, 1987

Stuffed Bell Peppers

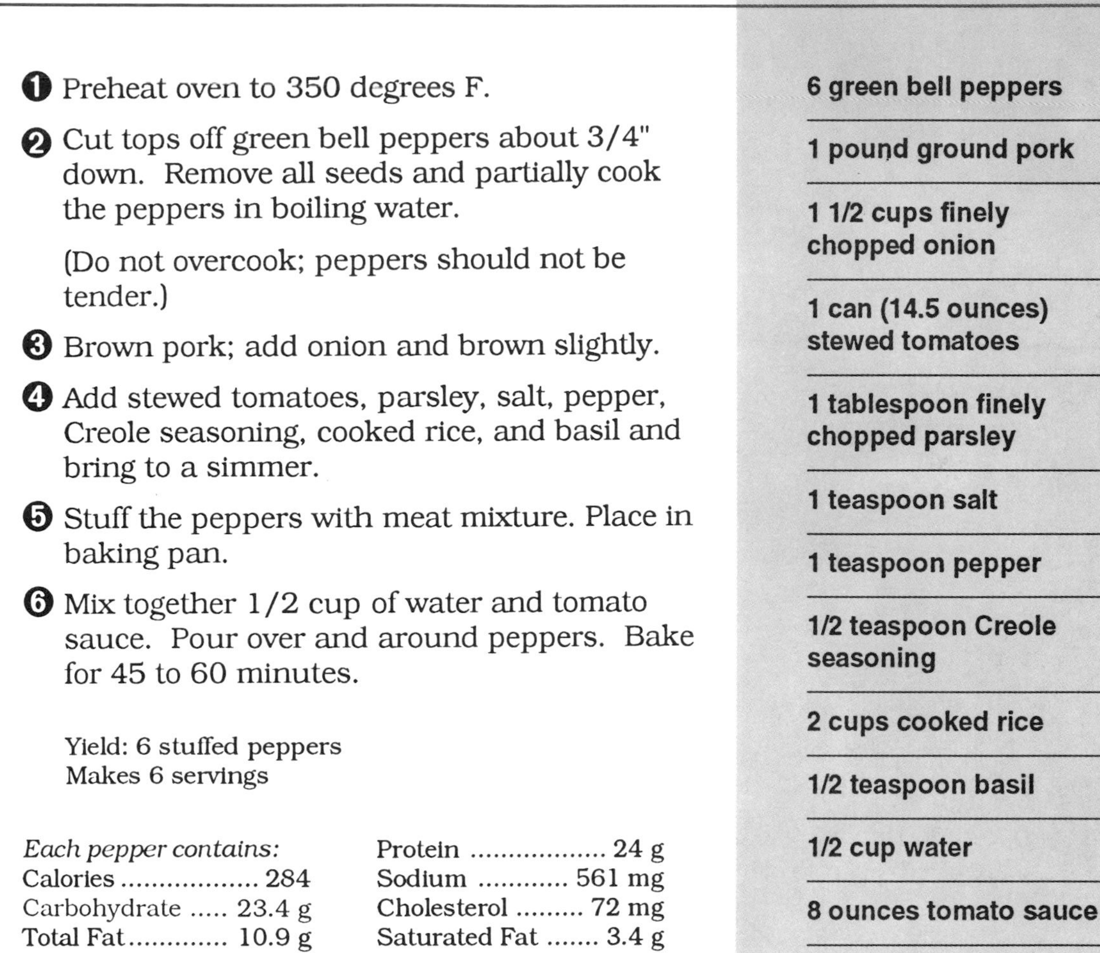

6 green bell peppers

1 pound ground pork

1 1/2 cups finely chopped onion

1 can (14.5 ounces) stewed tomatoes

1 tablespoon finely chopped parsley

1 teaspoon salt

1 teaspoon pepper

1/2 teaspoon Creole seasoning

2 cups cooked rice

1/2 teaspoon basil

1/2 cup water

8 ounces tomato sauce

1. Preheat oven to 350 degrees F.
2. Cut tops off green bell peppers about 3/4" down. Remove all seeds and partially cook the peppers in boiling water.

   (Do not overcook; peppers should not be tender.)
3. Brown pork; add onion and brown slightly.
4. Add stewed tomatoes, parsley, salt, pepper, Creole seasoning, cooked rice, and basil and bring to a simmer.
5. Stuff the peppers with meat mixture. Place in baking pan.
6. Mix together 1/2 cup of water and tomato sauce. Pour over and around peppers. Bake for 45 to 60 minutes.

Yield: 6 stuffed peppers
Makes 6 servings

Each pepper contains:

Calories	284	Protein	24 g
Carbohydrate	23.4 g	Sodium	561 mg
Total Fat	10.9 g	Cholesterol	72 mg
		Saturated Fat	3.4 g

Mrs. Oris Redlick
Grand Champion, 1987

Index

(By Title of Recipe)

Index

(By Kind of Food)

D

E

F

G

H

I

J

M

O

P

References

Acadiana Profile Magazine. (Lafayette, Louisiana. Volume 12, Number 2, Third Quarter 1985).

American Home Economics Association, *Handbook of Food Preparation*. 8th edition. (Alexandria, Virginia, 1980).

Cox, Beverly and Whitman, Joan. *Cooking Techniques*. (Boston/Toronto, 1981).

Davis, Frank. *The Frank Davis Seafood Notebook*. (Gretna, Louisiana, 1985).

Hoseney, R. Carl. *Principles of Cereal Science and Technology*. (St. Paul, Minnesota, 1986).

Hullah, Evelyn. *Cardinal's Handbook of Recipe Development*. (Ontario, Canada, 1984).

Igoe, Robert S. *Dictionary of Food Ingredients*. (New York, 1983).

Louisiana Cooperative Extension Service, *Louisiana Summary - Agricultural and Natural Resources - 1990*. (Baton Rouge, Louisiana).

Louisiana Life Magazine. (Metairie, Louisiana. January-February 1990, Volume 9, Number 6).

McClane, A. J. *The Encyclopedia of Fish Cookery*. (New York, 1977).

Morr, Mary L. and Irmiter, T. F. *Introductory Foods: A Laboratory Manual of Food Preparation and Evaluation*. 5th edition. (New York, 1990).

Riely, Elizabeth. *The Chef's Companion*. (New York, 1986).

Sultan, William J. *The Pastry Chef*. (Westport, Connecticut, 1983).

Webster's Ninth New Collegiate Dictionary. 9th edition. (Springfield, Massachusetts, 1983).

Company History

Lou Ana Foods began operating in 1894

For nearly 100 years vegetable oil has been produced on the same site in the small town of Opelousas in south-central Louisiana.

Lou Ana Foods, Inc. began in 1894 as the St. Landry Cotton Oil Company on land that was originally part of a Spanish land grant. Those were not easy years to begin a new enterprise and St. Landry Cotton Oil Company, which produced cottonseed oil for cooking and cottonseed meal for livestock, experienced hard times as a succession of people tried to make the venture go.

In 1919 a young man named J. P. Barnett joined the company, which had been idle for a short time and had reopened under the name of the Opelousas Cotton Oil Company. In 1924, Barnett bought the company, changed the name to the J. P. Barnett Company, and gave the operation a solid foundation that would serve it well for the next 47 years.

Under Barnett's direction, the company purchased its own cotton gins to assure the oil mill of sufficient sources of cotton seed for the crushing season.

Before and during the bleak years of the Depression, Barnett bought moss gins and broadened operations to include the ginning of Spanish moss for bedding and upholstery stuffing. Lines of horse-drawn wagons loaded with Spanish moss were a familiar sight outside the J. P. Barnett Company during this period, before the advent of synthetics.

The Depression left its mark on the company. In 1933 when President Roosevelt declared a bank "holiday" and closed all the banks, the J. P. Barnett Company was forced to suspend operations for a period. The company reopened with the Barnett family once again as owners and with a new name, Cotton Products Company.

The next 20 years were ones of growth. For example, in 1938 Barnett ordered construction of a vegetable oil refinery, an addition which, with the continual decline of cotton, eventually would become the most important operation of the company. Barnett probably didn't realize how farsighted his decision was, and how greatly the refinery would profit the company. It meant that not only could seeds be crushed into oil in Opelousas, but that now the oil could be refined there as well.

In 1938 Lou Ana began selling refined bulk oil to household name companies such as Procter and Gamble, Frito Lay, Jergens and Bristol-Myers Squibb Company. Packaged goods sales began in 1939 under the labels of Lou Ana and Perfecto to retail, institutional and concession distribution channels.

In 1971 Barnett retired as president when the company was sold. On July 16, 1971, the exact day and month in 1894 when the company was begun, Theodore G. Schad Jr., a native of Larchmont, N.Y., bought the Cotton Products Company. Schad, a former principal in the partnership and national director of marketing and economics for Peat, Marwick, Mitchell and Co., one of the nation's "Big Eight" accounting firms, changed the name to Lou Ana Foods, Inc. after his holding company, Schad Industries, Inc. (formerly Lou Ana Industries, Inc.) bought the company. Schad provided the expertise to lead the company into the 21st century.

Schad introduced modern sales and marketing techniques, expanded production capabilities, initiated export activities, modernized the firm's accounting procedures, entered the horticulture business, and developed a line of coatings as the beginning of an ingredients line.

Also under Schad's direction, a Total Quality Management Program was instituted, that bolstered the firm during the late 1980s' recession in the Louisiana oil patch. These techniques came directly from those taught by Dr. Deming, an American, to the Japanese back in the 1950s. In 1991 Lou Ana Foods reduced costs by $1,500,000 as a result of the program.

Lou Ana Foods, Inc. has won the State of Louisiana's Lantern Award for business excellence as well as the Business Achievement Award for Acadiana (south-central Louisiana).

Today Lou Ana Foods competes in the three broad segments of the vegetable oil refinery business: bulk/industrial, food service/concession, and retail.

Lou Ana Foods, Inc. is one of four companies operating under the umbrella of Schad Industries, Inc. All of the corporations, including Lou Ana Foods of Texas, Lou Ana Gardens and Schad Industries International, are focusing on the future and meeting the complex needs of today's and tomorrow's consumers.

To order LOUISIANA FESTIVALS COOKBOOK (BOOK 1), fill out this form (or a photocopy of it), clip it out and mail it with your remittance to: Lou Ana Gardens, Inc., P.O. Drawer 53247, Lafayette, LA 70505. To order by phone, call 1-800-259-3355.

'es! Please send me ________ copies of "Louisiana ivals Cookbook (Book 1)" @ $24.45 each, postpaid.
derstand that it is $24.45 per copy, which covers 95 for the book and $2.50 for shipping. (Louisiana lents add $1.65 for sales tax.)

nclosed is my check or money order for $________.
d rather charge it. Please charge $_________
my ❑ VISA ❑ MC
#

________ ________________________
ation Signature

n interested in obtaining "Louisiana Festivals Cook- (Book 2)." Please notify me when it is available.

____
YOUR NAME

____
ADDRESS

____
CITY, STATE, ZIP

• Check, money order or credit card authorization must accompany order • Make check payable to Lou Ana Gardens • No CODs • Add $3.00 per copy for out-of-U.S. orders

❑ If you are buying books for someone besides yourself (or in addition to yourself), please check here and write the name and address of the recipient(s) on a separate sheet of paper and mail it along with this order form.

- -

To order LOUISIANA FESTIVALS COOKBOOK (BOOK 1), fill out this form (or a photocopy of it), clip it out and mail it with your remittance to: Lou Ana Gardens, Inc., P.O. Drawer 53247, Lafayette, LA 70505. To order by phone, call 1-800-259-3355.

s! Please send me ________ copies of "Louisiana vals Cookbook (Book 1)" @ $24.45 each, postpaid.
erstand that it is $24.45 per copy, which covers 5 for the book and $2.50 for shipping. (Louisiana nts add $1.65 for sales tax.)

closed is my check or money order for $________.
rather charge it. Please charge $_________
my ❑ VISA ❑ MC
#

________ ________________________
tion Signature

interested in obtaining "Louisiana Festivals Cook- Book 2)." Please notify me when it is available.

____
YOUR NAME

____
ADDRESS

____
CITY, STATE, ZIP

• Check, money order or credit card authorization must accompany order • Make check payable to Lou Ana Gardens • No CODs • Add $3.00 per copy for out-of-U.S. orders

❑ If you are buying books for someone besides yourself (or in addition to yourself), please check here and write the name and address of the recipient(s) on a separate sheet of paper and mail it along with this order form.

To order LOUISIANA FESTIVALS COOKBOOK (BOOK 1), fill out this form (or a photocopy of it), clip it out and mail it with your remittance to: Lou Ana Gardens, Inc., P.O. Drawer 53247, Lafayette, LA 70505. To order by phone, call 1-800-259-3355.

Yes! Please send me ________ copies of "Louisiana stivals Cookbook (Book 1)" @ $24.45 each, postpaid. nderstand that it is $24.45 per copy, which covers 1.95 for the book and $2.50 for shipping. (Louisiana idents add $1.65 for sales tax.)

Enclosed is my check or money order for $________.
I'd rather charge it. Please charge $__________
to my ❑ VISA ❑ MC
CT # ☐☐☐☐☐☐☐☐☐☐☐☐☐☐☐☐

________ iration   ____________________ Signature

'm interested in obtaining "Louisiana Festivals Cook-k (Book 2)." Please notify me when it is available.

____
YOUR NAME

____
ADDRESS

____
CITY, STATE, ZIP

• Check, money order or credit card authorization must accompany order • Make check payable to Lou Ana Gardens • No CODs • Add $3.00 per copy for out-of-U.S. orders

❑ If you are buying books for someone besides yourself (or in addition to yourself), please check here and write the name and address of the recipient(s) on a separate sheet of paper and mail it along with this order form.

- -

To order LOUISIANA FESTIVALS COOKBOOK (BOOK 1), fill out this form (or a photocopy of it), clip it out and mail it with your remittance to: Lou Ana Gardens, Inc., P.O. Drawer 53247, Lafayette, LA 70505. To order by phone, call 1-800-259-3355.

'es! Please send me ________ copies of "Louisiana tivals Cookbook (Book 1)" @ $24.45 each, postpaid. derstand that it is $24.45 per copy, which covers 95 for the book and $2.50 for shipping. (Louisiana lents add $1.65 for sales tax.)

nclosed is my check or money order for $________.
d rather charge it. Please charge $__________
my ❑ VISA ❑ MC
☐☐☐☐☐☐☐☐☐☐☐☐☐☐☐☐

________ ation   ____________________ Signature

n interested in obtaining "Louisiana Festivals Cook- (Book 2)." Please notify me when it is available.

____
YOUR NAME

____
ADDRESS

____
CITY, STATE, ZIP

• Check, money order or credit card authorization must accompany order • Make check payable to Lou Ana Gardens • No CODs • Add $3.00 per copy for out-of-U.S. orders

❑ If you are buying books for someone besides yourself (or in addition to yourself), please check here and write the name and address of the recipient(s) on a separate sheet of paper and mail it along with this order form.